Exploring History
in the
Scottish Borders

Ian Douglas

Dedication

Dedicated to Angela, who persuaded me that a book on the history of the Borders was needed, and to Caroline, for her help in editing the book. But I didn't always take her advice, and any errors are mine!

Copyright

Please see the author's website **www.theheritagephotographer.com** for regular updates and details of other publications.

Cover photograph Smailholm Tower northwest of Kelso.
Back page photograph Hadrian's Wall west of Housesteads Fort.

Exploring History in the Scottish Borders

Contents

LIST OF PHOTOGRAPHS AND ILLUSTRATIONS

Cover photograph Smailholm Tower northwest of Kelso.
Back page photograph Hadrian's Wall west of Housesteads Fort.

PREFACE

The Scottish border area is steeped in history. This is the crossroads between the north and south of Britain. The often fraught relationship between England and Scotland left its mark. Centuries of war and bloodshed didn't produce Robin Hood characters, it produced a tough and often violent people, the border reivers. In the 16th century the Scottish borderland made the American Wild West of the 19th century look like a kindergarten.

"Exploring History in the Scottish Borders" provides an overview of the history of this turbulent area. The Borders' past has left a legacy of splendid castles, beautiful ruined abbeys, and a depth of history few other areas can match. This book tells the story of the of the English/Scottish borderland from the time of the Romans, through the Scottish wars of independence, the turbulent 16th century and Henry VIII's "rough wooing", up until the reopening of part of the Waverley Line by Queen Elizabeth in 2015.

But after centuries of conflict what was once the most violent part of the UK is now one of the most peaceful. It is a great place to visit - for many visitors it has more to offer than the nearby Lake District. Like the Lake District the Borders has beautiful countryside and strong literary connections, but the Borders also has a depth of history that the Lakes just cannot rival. It is also much less crowded and commercialized.

Structure of the Book

Chapter 1 provides a very brief history of Scotland, with special reference to the Borders.

Chapter 2 describes Hadrian's Wall, an early attempt to define a border, and a World Heritage site.

Chapter 3 focuses on the border reivers, the gangsters of the Borders.

Chapter 4 describes many of the Borders' strategic fortifications, and the smaller fortified buildings such as pele towers and bastle houses which provided protection in this turbulent land.

Chapter 5 covers the jewels of the Borders, its abbeys, and other religious monuments.

Chapter 6 covers the stately homes of the Borders, and discusses Sir Walter Scott's achievements.

Chapter 7 overviews the Border railways which once brought so many communities together, and welcomes the reopening of part of the Waverley Line in 2015.

Chapter 8 will help if you are planning a visit, and suggests an itinerary for visiting the main sites. Postcodes of the key sites are used throughout the text, to help visitors with smartphones or satellite navigation systems in their cars, and preplanning on google maps. Two paper maps are recommended in the bibliography.

Chapter 9 provides an overview of the main Scottish Border surnames, as I suspect many readers will have family links with the area.

Many of the photographs in the book can be obtained from www.picfair.com, for printing on your printer, sending to a commercial printer or using as a screen saver. Just search for Ian Douglas in the website's search box. Click on the photo to see the full photo.

November 2015

1. EXPLORING HISTORY IN THE SCOTTISH BORDERS

And how the Borders became a "Failed State" in the 16th Century.

The Romans

The most well-known attempt to create a barrier between the north and the south of the island of Britain was made 1900 years ago. Hadrian's Wall runs for seventy four miles (119 km) from Bo'ness-on-Solway, which is west of Carlisle, to the appropriately named Wallsend, east of Newcastle. Built on the orders of Emperor Hadrian from 122AD to 128AD, it was intended to define the end of the civilized world, with Scotland on the other side! It was only partially successful in keeping the "barbarians" out, and was overrun on several occasions.

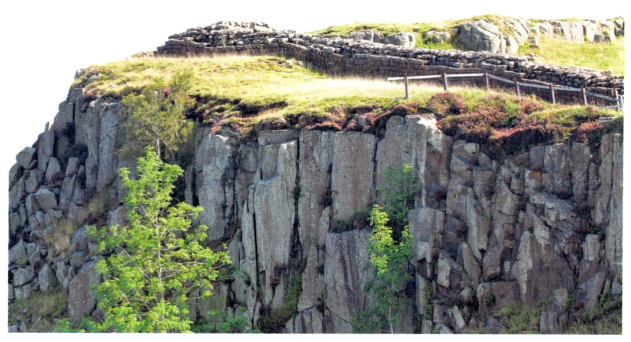

1. Hadrian's Wall following a naturally defensive position on the Walltown Crags.

The wall has fifteen forts, eighty-one milecastles (Roman miles were slightly shorter than our miles), and two turrets between each milecastles. Forts could usually hold up to a thousand men when they were at full complement. Milecastles were garrisoned with twenty to thirty solders, who controlled gates through the wall. The turrets were watchtowers, and probably held about eight men. The main garrison was stationed in the large forts situated along the wall, or slightly behind it. Hadrian's Wall is covered in more detail in chapter 2.

After the Romans

In about 410AD the Romans pulled their forces out of England and Wales. That left the inhabitants vulnerable – they had become very dependent on a professional army for defense. In the century following the Roman withdrawal the Angles, a Germanic tribe, invaded Northumberland, the English county on the east coast just south of the Border. The Angles created a kingdom they called Bernicia.

The Angles originated from southern Denmark and northern Germany, and spoke a German dialect. The Scottish dialect retains closer links to the language spoken by the Angles than southern English does, as the Scottish dialect has not had the same level of input from the Norman French spoken by William the Conqueror as southern English has. The Normans, like the Romans, weren't able to successfully maintain a significant presence in Scotland.

By the early 7th century the Angles in the kingdom of Bernicia had extended their control into what is now the Scottish Borders, as far west as Dumfriesshire, and as far north as Lothian up to the Firth of Forth. Then the pagan Bernician king was killed in battle by the rival Anglian king of East Anglia in 616 or 617. His sons were taken for their safety by their father's supporters to the Christian Gaelic kingdom of Dal Riata in Scotland, where they were brought up as Christians.

After sixteen years they regained their father's kingdom of Bernicia and under their leadership the kingdom, which included the Borders, became Christian. By the 670's the kingdom had become the dominant force in Britain. At that time there was no Scottish/English border. Northumberland and the Borders were at the very centre of political, religious, artistic and scholarly life. The religious houses of Melrose, Lindisfarne and Jarrow were beacons of learning. Around 700 the Lindisfarne Gospels was produced in the priory of Lindisfarne, a truly beautiful book of the gospels and religious text, which can be viewed on the British Library's website (http://www.bl.uk/onlinegallery/sacredtexts/lindisfarne.html). Jarrow was the monastery of the venerable Bede, and where in around 731 he completed the Historia Ecclesiastica Gentis Anglorum, or An Ecclesiastical History of the English People. Most historians consider this to be the most important original reference on Anglo-Saxon history. The Ruthwell and Bewcastle crosses (see Chapter 5) help to demonstrate the geographical spread and sophistication of their culture.

In 685, when the Bernician kingdom under King Ecgfrith was at its peak, Ecgfrith overstretched himself. He led a punitive raid against the Picts. The Picts lured his army deep into Pictish territory and then ambushed it at Dunnichen near Forfar, destroying the army and killing Ecgfrith. After that the Bernician Empire was slowly chipped away by its neighbors to the north and south.

In 793 the Viking raids started, with the first raid in the British Isles on Lindisfarne (also known as Holy Isle). Lindisfarne is an island just off the Northumbrian coast, about 15 miles (24 km) south of the current border, and is joined to the mainland by a causeway at low tide. During the next 200 years Northumbria (at that time extending as far north as Edinburgh) was subject to Danish Viking raids, and the south of Northumbria was invaded and ruled by the Danes. At their peak the Danes controlled all of England except Wessex. However, the fact that our language is based on Anglian, rather than Danish, is one indication that the local population was not wiped out, albeit the Danes almost certainly took over the best and most productive land in the areas they controlled.

In the 900s Northumbria controlled the eastern Borders and Lothians up to the Firth of Forth, and had done so for three centuries. However the Scots, then established north of the Firth of Forth, became more aggressive. In the 950's they took Edinburgh. Around 973 Northumbria was forced to relinquish further territory in Lothian to the Scots.

But the Scots wanted more, they saw Northumberland as much theirs as anyone else's. The Scots made a number of raids into England. In 1006, for example, they besieged Durham. On this occasion they were beaten, and the women of Durham were given a cow each for cleaning and preparing the heads of dead Scottish soldiers for display around the walls of the city!

In 1018 the Scots under their king Malcolm II won a great victory over the Northumbrians at Carham, just south of the River Tweed and west of Coldstream. This established the Tweed as the new Scottish/English border in the east.

A momentous event in the history of this British Isles was the Norman invasion in 1066. It took the Normans several decades to pacify England and Wales. At the same time they were dealing with Scottish raids. By 1092 King Rufus, William the Conqueror's son and successor, had taken over Cumbria and its capital Carlisle. Before the takeover Cumbria had been ruled by a chieftain who considered the Scottish king as his overlord. So as Cumbria was part of Scotland when the Domesday Book was compiled in the 1080s, it was not included in the Domesday Book. Rufus's successful invasion of Cumbria created the Solway as the western border between England and Scotland, and although Scotland occupied Cumbria on occasions after that, Scotland was not able to hold onto it in the long-term.

Scotland then had almost 200 years of relative peace. Relative, that is, to what came later – in this period of relative peace there were still several major conflicts. The English and Scottish royal families were related by marriage, and the Scottish royal family had significant land holdings in England. So they got involved in some English kingship succession disputes and power struggles. On one occasion England controlled much of the Borders area. They had obtained this as part of a ransom for the Scottish King, William I, who had been captured at Alnwick when he was leading an ill-judged raid into England. Richard the Lionheart sold the Borders back to Scotland to help pay for his crusade to the Holy Land.

The border has changed many times since Hadrian, with much of Northumberland and Cumbria being in Scotland in the 11th century. However, the border settled to just north of Carlisle in the west, and to the lower reaches of the River Tweed in the east, in the 12th century.

I said earlier that the Normans had not successfully invaded Scotland. In the later part of the 13th century

2. Edward I's statue at Burgh by Sands where he died.

Edward I, the English king, decided to try. The Scottish king, Alexander III, had died and shortly afterwards Alexander's direct heir died. Alexander's first wife, who had predeceased him, was Edward's sister, and relations with England had been good. Alexander's reign had been a long, prosperous and relatively peaceful one. But things were about to change.

Edward, soon to be called the Hammer of the Scots, saw an opportunity and tried to become the overlord of Scotland. To cut a long story short, Edward was asked by the Scottish guardians, who were responsible for Scotland in the absence of a monarch, to mediate between the thirteen claimants to the Scottish throne.

This was inviting the fox into the henhouse. Edward supported John Balliol, probably the strongest contender for the throne, provided that he accepted Edward as his overlord. This resulted in a civil war in Scotland between the supporters of Balliol and Bruce (the other main contender), and a war between Scotland and England.

Edward 1 died in 1307 of dysentery whilst at Burgh by Sands on the Solway coast, preparing his army for yet another invasion of Scotland. He was aged 68 and worn out by campaigning. Edward was succeeded by his divisive and incompetent son Edward II. In 1314 at the Battle of Bannockburn near Stirling the Scots soundly defeated Edward II. Bannockburn was a massive success for the Scots, and is the one battle all Scots remember, just as English football supporters remember the 1966 World Cup, the one World Cup England won! However Bannockburn was not the end of the war.

As we discussed earlier, the Scottish border is in many respects simply a political construct. Unlike many borders the peoples on both sides are ethnically the same, and speak the same language, albeit with some differences in accent as you get further away from the border line. For much of the 14th to the 16th centuries Borderers saw themselves as neither really English nor Scots, but acted in their own, or their family's or clan's interests, rather than in a "national" interest. These were ruthless and violent people living in a very violent time. As Sir Walter Scott wrote in his poem Marmion:

> "Let Nobles fight for fame;
> Let vassals follow where they lead,
> Burghers to guard their townships bleed,
> But war's the borderers' game.
> Their gain, their glory, their delight,
> To sleep the day, maraud the night
> O'er mountain, moss, and moor;
> Joyful to fight they took their way,
> Scarce caring who won the day,
> Their booty was secure."

Whilst I abhor their involvement in war and pillaging, I can't help but respect the Borderers for their rejection of jingoism and nationalism. As Samuel Johnston, the 18th century critic and compiler of the first English dictionary observed, patriotism is often the last refuge of a scoundrel. And of course with the surname of Johnston, his family may well have originated in the Borders!

But what is the back-story to this? Why did many borderers become the gangsters of the 16th century, self-reliant, brutal and warlike, with allegiance to neither Scotland nor England?

In the decades after Bannockburn invading English armies or raiding parties marched through the Borders on several occasions, and Scottish armies returned the favor in raids and reprisal attacks deep into England. As the English invaders passed through, the retreating Scots laid waste to the Borders to rob the invaders of anything to live on. The invaders raped and pillaged, and tried to live off what they could steal. I don't imagine the Scots forces were any better. The area became a battleground. It created a population desensitized to violence, and led to 300 years of lawlessness in the Borders. In many ways the history of Afghanistan is similar, although Afghanistan's troubles started far earlier.

The strategic city and port of Berwick-upon-Tweed, on the north bank of the Tweed, changed hands thirteen times in the bloody two centuries after it was captured by Edward I in 1296. Finally in 1482 it settled in England permanently, a bit of a Border's anomaly as the rest of the north bank of the Tweed is Scottish territory.

Berwick-upon-Tweed's English status undoubtedly held back the economic development of the Scottish eastern border area, as the main port was for much of the time under the control of a foreign and unfriendly power. This was one of the reasons the once significant Border's town of Roxburgh in Scotland declined – it was no longer able to import or export through its most convenient port. Roxburgh was once very important, and is one of only six Scottish towns recorded on the Mappa Mundi, a map of the world as then known, drawn up about 1300 and now considered a medieval treasure. The Mappa Mundi is on display in Hereford Cathedral. The former medieval town of Roxburgh no longer exists, but its name is now used by a small and attractive village about two miles (3 km) from the site of this once important town.

The Borders in the 16th Century

The Borders has been the site of many English/Scottish battles. The one that can't be missed from an overview of Border's history is Flodden. The battle was fought just a few miles on the English side of the border, actually by the village of Branxton two miles (3 km) from Flodden. The battle was the opposite of Bannockburn; the English army won at Flodden, and won decisively.

Flodden took place in 1513, one hundred and ninety nine years after Bannockburn. The Scots under James IV had invaded England in support of their French allies. The English king, Henry VIII of the many wives, was fighting with the main English army in France in an attempt to take over all of France. Therefore France wanted to create a second front by encouraging the Scots to invade England.

The Scottish invasion was contrary to the "Treaty of Perpetual Peace" signed between Scotland and England in 1502. However, there were tensions between the two countries as Henry VIII had made attempts to belittle the Scottish king – Henry wanted the King of Scotland as his vassal, rather than an equal. France was also Scotland's long standing ally, and offered Scotland money to become involved in the war. This was particularly attractive to a Scottish king whose coffers were low.

As the main English army was fighting in France under Henry VIII, to meet the Scottish invasion a "second division" English army was put together under the elderly but highly competent and experienced Earl of Surrey. England had some time to do this, as in accordance with his understanding of medieval chivalry king James IV of Scotland wrote to the English king giving him a month's notice of his intention to invade!

The Scottish army crossed the Tweed near Coldstream and travelled several miles on the English side of the Border, taking and occupying the English castles of Norham and Etal. At Etal Lady Heron had been in charge of the castle and was a beautiful but wicked woman, according to Robert Lindsay of Pitscottie, a contemporary and a historian. She may have seduced James, and a tryst would explain why the Scottish army was delayed for some days, giving their enemies more time to mobilize.

Estimates are that the Scottish army was about 30,000, outnumbering the English army of 22,000. The Scots took up an excellent defensive position but then, at the request of the Earl of Surrey who appealed to the Scot's chivalry, moved from this position to attack the English army. I find the concept of chivalry in battle difficult to understand, when the whole purpose of a battle is to hack the enemy to pieces, to me a barbarous rather than a chivalric act! However, the late medieval mind seemed to be able to comprehend this chivalric concept.

When the Scots attacked in serried ranks they became bogged down in the unexpectedly marshy ground, which made them very vulnerable to the English, who were on slightly higher ground. But it was also a victory for the key English weapon, the bill. This was a relatively short weapon, about six foot or so long (two metres), with a chopping blade and several protruding spikes on the blade. The Scots used the pike, just as they had at Bannockburn 199 years before. The pike was a 15 foot (about five metres) spear, designed for thrusting rather than throwing. The bill was a very effective weapon in the close combat of Flodden, as it could break the shaft of the pike, leaving Scottish soldiers with sticks to fight with!

The battle was a disaster for Scotland. James IV and much of the Scottish nobility were killed – at least they led from the front. It was a battle where no quarter was given. Figures differ, but many historians estimate that about ten thousand Scots were killed, and four thousand English, in two and a half hour of bloody hand-to-hand fighting.

James IV's heir, James V, was only 17 months old at the time. Therefore the battle resulted in a minor being nominally in charge of Scotland, a common occurrence in Scottish history. Luckily for Scotland Henry VIII was preoccupied with France and therefore did not take the opportunity to try to take over Scotland, although he certainly tried later.

Thomas Ruthall, Bishop of Durham, who was present at the battle, wrote to Cardinal Thomas Wolsey, Henry's adviser and fixer, with details of the conflict. He wrote that when the English army was away from their tents fighting the Scots, all their goods, horses and belongings were stolen by the borderers. This may well have been true – it was certainly true to type!

The remainder of the 16th century continued in the bloody traditions of Flodden.

At a national political level there were several reasons for friction between Scotland and England. Until 1560 Scotland was allied with France, which saw and used Scotland as a "second front" in its disputes with England. Secondly, although England and Scotland eventually became Protestant, they did so at different speeds and in different forms, so for part of the century there were major religious differences. And lastly, and by no means least, Henry VIII wanted to take over Scotland, or at least make the Scottish king subservient to him.

Henry VIII had two main problems: he needed to produce a son to continue his dynasty (he is well known for his little "marital difficulties"); and he was financially broke. The Catholic Church in England had an income of £300,000 a year – the English state's income was £100,000, and Henry needed money to fund his lifestyle and his off and on war with France.

Henry came up with a wheeze which he hoped would solve both his problems. In 1535 he "deposed" the Pope as head of the English church. The Pope was getting in Henry's way by refusing him permission to divorce his wife Catherine, which would have allowed Henry to marry Anne Boleyn, an attractive young woman of child-bearing age, unlike Catherine. So Henry appointed himself head of the Church in England, which dispensed with the need for him to get the Pope's permission to divorce Catherine, and gave him access to the church's very substantial property and funds. The corruption that had been endemic in some parts of the church helped to justify Henry's takeover. The Church of England then increasingly over the following decades became a Protestant church, with the abolition of mass and clerical celibacy, and the move from Latin to English for services. In Scotland Protestantism, in a more radical form than the English version, was on the rise too, but it took Scotland about 25 years longer to become officially Protestant.

By 1542 King James V of Scotland was 30. Unfortunately relations between England and Scotland had broken down again. Henry VIII had invited James to a meeting at York to discuss his religious policy. But on the advice of his counselors James didn't turn up. Henry was incensed by this insult, and saw James as being in league with the Pope, which many historians believe was probably true.

Hostilities intensified. There were a number of border incidents. Henry VIII sent an army into Scotland to teach James a lesson, but this was beaten by the Scots at the battle of Haddon Rig near Kelso in August 1542, and it withdrew.

In retaliation for Henry's ill-fated raid into Scotland, James decided that Scotland should raid into England, and he assembled an army of at least 15,000. Making its way towards Carlisle, at Solway Moss the Scottish army was met by an English force of about 3,000. The English force was largely made up of reivers under the command of the English Warden, Henry's key official in the area. There was a big difference in the quality of leadership of the armies, and this was to prove decisive. The English force was competently commanded. The Scots were commanded by Sir Oliver Sinclair of Pitcairn, James's favorite. But Sinclair was disliked and his leadership was not accepted by many of the Scots magnates. So the Scottish force's command was disunited and morale was low.

The battle was a disaster for Scotland. The Scots were outmaneuvered and hemmed in by the English army. One estimate is that only 12 Scots and 7 English were killed in the battle, but 1,200 Scots were taken prisoner, and several hundred Scots were drowned in the River Esk trying to escape. Solway Moss was very different to the battle of Flodden under James' father – at Flodden the Scots were prepared to fight to the death, and many did so. At Solway Moss they had no confidence in the Scottish leadership and were not prepared to die.

James, who had been at Lochmaben Castle in the Borders while the fighting took place, retired a broken man to his palace at Falkland in Fife. He was already suffering from a fever, possible cholera, and died there aged 30, just 7 days after his wife gave birth to a daughter. The daughter was Mary, Queen of Scots, who must rival Robert the Bruce as the most famous of the Scottish monarchs.

With the King dead and the Scottish army broken, Henry VIII could probably have taken Scotland by force if he wanted to. But, perhaps aware that winning Scotland by force was one thing, holding it indefinitely against guerrilla warfare was another, Henry came up with a "cunning plan". Henry wanted his five years old son Edward, (Henry had fathered a son by then), to marry the infant Mary when they were of age. That would give Henry and his dynasty control of Scotland.

In 1543, after much politicking by Henry, the six month old Mary was contracted by the Scottish parliament to marry Prince Edward when she was ten. However, the Catholic faction in Scotland thought better of this. The Catholic political faction, led by Mary's staunchly Catholic mother, was very powerful at that time and did not want its queen to marry a Protestant monarch. Scottish sentiment in general turned against the marriage to a future king of England, which would have led to England controlling Scotland. Therefore the marriage contract was annulled, much to Henry's fury.

This resulted in what became known as the "rough wooing". To terrorize the Scots and obtain their agreement to the marriage, Henry sent armies into Scotland. There followed eight years of conflict and devastation, particularly in the Borders. In May 1544 a large English army invaded and laid waste to Edinburgh, although the castle managed to hold out. Henry's official, Wharton, used bribery and threat to turn many of the Scottish reiving families against one another, creating a civil war in the Borders.

In the end it achieved nothing except destruction. The young Mary was sent to France in July 1547 for her own safety, and to become the wife of the French Dauphin, that is the prince who was heir to the throne of France. Two months after Mary left, a large English army defeated the Scots at the battle of Pinkie near Musselburgh, east of Edinburgh. Shortly afterward the Scots, bolstered by French Catholic troops, got the better of the English army, and managed to besiege them in the East Lothian town of Haddington

And so it went on. Henry VIII reinforced his invading troops, and for several years much of southern Scotland was controlled by England. It was a ghastly time of guerrilla warfare, retaliation and atrocities. Eventually England decided that controlling Scotland was not worth the cost, and a treaty was agreed.

In the 1550s in order to bolster its defenses against the English, Mary's mother, the French aristocrat Mary de Guise-Lorraine who ruled Scotland for some of this period, asked the French king to send troops to assist the Scots. Scotland had become a client of France.

But amongst all this a religious revolution was fermenting in Scotland. In 1560 Scotland officially became Protestant, after decades of dispute and struggle between the two versions of Christianity. In one of the bizarre twists of history this made Scotland, up to a point at least, an ally of Protestant England, rather than Catholic France. Catholic France had troops based in Scotland which it was reluctant to withdraw. The Scottish parliament had to get help from England to evict them! Politics can be so strange.

But what of Mary, Queen of Scots? Unfortunately only a year after he had become King of France, Mary's young husband died of an ear infection. In 1561 Mary returned to Scotland as Queen of Scots, as her marriage contract (yes, royalty had pre-nups in the 16th century), did not allow her to remain as Queen of France in the event of her husband's death. She returned still staunchly Catholic to a country that only the year before had become Protestant, and which had significant religious tensions between the Catholic minority and the Protestant majority and the state.

3. Because of concerns about a Scottish invasion, in the 1560s Berwick-upon-Tweed's land-facing walls were replaced with a mile and a quarter (2 km) of the latest artillery fortifications.

It would take a book, and there are many of them, to describe Mary's reign. In the briefest summary, Mary made an unsuitable marriage to the unpleasant and immature Lord Darnley, had a child by him, the future James VI, and was implicated in Darnley's murder – a possible but unproven charge. Mary retained her Catholic faith, which caused nothing but conflict in Scotland. She had an affair with and married Lord Bothwell, who was almost certainly involved in Darnley's murder. She was imprisoned by the Scottish nobles, but escaped to England, where she was held under "protective custody" by her cousin Queen Elizabeth I. Mary conspired with Catholic nobles in England against Elizabeth, and therefore Elizabeth eventually had her executed. Through all of this time the Borders was a centre of anarchy. But this requires its own chapter – see chapter 3.

The 17th and 18th Centuries

It all changed in the early 17th century. Queen Elizabeth I of England died childless on 24 March 1603 at Richmond Palace (which no longer exists). Robert Carey, a former English March Warden, that is the monarch's official responsible for law and order and security in the Borders, had come to London when Elizabeth's death was anticipated. Carey wanted to be the first to tell James VI of Scotland of Elizabeth's death.

James had a kingdom to gain. Elizabeth's death ended the direct line of the English monarchy from Henry VIII, as Henry's other children had also died childless. However in 1503, 100 years before Elizabeth died, Henry's older sister Margaret Tudor had married James IV of Scotland. Henry VIII's sister was therefore James VI great grandmother, through James V, and Mary, Queen of Scots. That made James VI first in line to inherit the English throne.

Carey's sister, Lady Scrope, was one of Queen Elizabeth's attendants. As a sign of Elizabeth's death she is reputed to have dropped the queen's sapphire ring, a present to Elizabeth from King James, out of the palace window to Carey. Carey then rode the 400 miles (645 kilometres) from London to Edinburgh in about 60 hours – he had fresh mounts positioned along the route. He brought the Scottish king news that he was now King of England and Scotland, and Elizabeth's ring would have helped to prove it. James could therefore act quickly, and this helped to pre-empt any attempts by other factions in London to favor other candidates.

James VI of Scotland's accession to the English throne as James 1 of England changed the politics of the Borders totally. James VI and I saw the Borders as the middle of the country, not the end – he referred to the Borders as the middle shires. He had the will, the motive, and having the English treasury at his disposal he had the money to pacify the area. He appointed competent and ruthless officers to govern the Borders. They had no hesitation in organising the execution of the more prominent reivers – there were plenty of charges that could be laid against them. The luckier ones were sent to the Low Countries to fight the Spanish, or to Northern Ireland as part of the "plantation" of Protestant Scots amongst the Catholic Irish by King James. Many of their Borders estates were confiscated and sold at knockdown prices. By 1610 the day of the border reiver was nearing an end.

But the 17th century wasn't entirely peaceful. The 17th century saw much religious strife, between the very Presbyterian Scottish government and the supporters of the crown. King Charles I, the son of James VI and actually born in Scotland, wanted to introduce an Episcopalian form of church governance to the church in Scotland. This involved having bishops and religious practices similar to those of the Church of England imposed on the Scottish church. This was an anathema to the Scots. An important figure in this complicated period was the Marquis of Montrose, who led a small army that wreaked havoc across the north of Scotland, before being beaten in battle at Philiphaugh, just outside Selkirk in the Borders. Although Montrose escaped on this occasion, he was later caught and hung, drawn and quartered in Edinburgh. Scotland still used this barbaric form of execution.

Charles I was eventually beheaded by the English, having been handed over to them by the Scots, with whom he sought refuge after his defeat in the Civil War. The Scottish government was very unhappy about the execution, as Charles was King of Scotland as well as England. But, as Neil Oliver points out in his book "A History of Scotland", it was not possible to behead the King of England without beheading the King of Scotland!

Later the strongly Presbyterian faction in Scotland had Charles I's son crowned King of Scotland as they had an agreement with him that their austere version of Christianity would be imposed throughout England and Ireland if he became king. The English parliament saw this as a threat and so, as a pre-emptive strike, parliament instructed Oliver Cromwell to invade Scotland. Again the Borders were laid waste, before the Scottish army was soundly beaten at the Battle of Dunbar, half way between Berwick-upon-Tweed and Edinburgh, in September 1650.

After Oliver Cromwell's death Charles I's son was invited back to be king of England and Scotland as Charles II.

The Stewart family, which was the family of the James and Charles kings, had ruled Scotland for several centuries, and England from 1603, with an interlude following the civil war. But in 1688 they were deposed because of their Catholic sympathies, and replaced by William of Orange.

In the 18th century, the Stewart's supporters, the Jacobites as they were known, made several attempts to win back the throne. So in 1715 the Borders again became an invasion route. A Jacobite army from Scotland bypassed the castle of Carlisle, but proclaimed James Stewart king in Brampton, an attractive English border town near Carlisle, before they were soundly beaten at Preston. The second major attempt was in 1745. Bonnie Prince Charlie, Charles Stewart, landed in the Highlands from France and invaded England via the west coast, taking Carlisle Castle and garrisoning it. When he retreated, Carlisle Castle was besieged by the pursuing government forces, and was eventually forced to surrender because the medieval walls were no match for 18th century artillery.

From Sir Walter Scott to Today

What happened to the Borders after that? They spawned one of the UK's most successful writers in the 19th century. Sir Walter Scott, although born in Edinburgh, was from a Borders family and chose to spend much of his life there. Scott's life and contribution to Scotland are discussed in chapter 6.

The Borders has successful agricultural and tourist industries. It also developed a very successful knitwear and woolen industry, particularly in Galashiels, Hawick and Selkirk, because of an abundance of sheep to provide wool and water power to power the looms. Water power was essential for largescale manufacturing before coal power became the norm. However this industry has shrunk in recent decades as production moved to lower cost countries. This resulted in high levels of unemployment and left some empty, decaying mills which are not an asset to their communities. The industry now concentrates on small volume, high quality textiles.

But after centuries of conflict what was once the most violent part of the UK is now one of the most peaceful.

The Borders and the World

The border families have had a very great impact on the world. The Johnstones and Nixons went on to produce Presidents of the United States in the 20th century, and a borderer from Selkirk was a maternal ancestor of Franklin D Roosevelt. The Armstrongs produced the first man on the moon. The Borders' contribution to science is often overlooked. James Clerk Maxwell was one of the greatest physicists of the 19th century, and was brought up and lived when he could in a family estate near Dalbeattie in the western Borders. Lord Rutherford, who made an enormous contribution to nuclear physics in the early 20th century, was born in New Zealand but was clearly of a border family. Another Rutherford, Daniel Rutherford, discovered nitrogen in Edinburgh in 1772. Daniel Rutherford's half-sister was the mother of Sir Walter Scott, the author. Scott also played a major part in documenting, and some would argue embellishing, border and Scottish culture. As well as Scott, James Hogg, the son of an Ettrick shepherd, is a world-class author.

Quite an achievement for such a small area!

2. HADRIAN'S WALL

4. The Wall west of Housesteads Fort.

Before the Wall

The Romans successfully invaded Britain in 43 AD, after short-lived invasions in 55 BC and 54 BC. They proceeded, using a mixture of diplomacy and military victories, to move north. In about 71AD they invaded what is now Scotland. They may have won a great victory over the Scottish tribes at a place the Roman historian Tacitus calls Mons Graupius. The exact site of Mons Graupius is not known, but is likely to be in the north east of Scotland. However some historians now doubt the scale of the battle, and believe that this could have been greatly embellished by Tacitus and the Roman governor, Agricola, to impress the emperor. Tacitus was Agricola's son-in-law, and therefore had a vested interest in embellishing Agricola's achievements. Whatever the truth is, at their peak the Romans had forts in the Scottish lowlands and up the east coast of Scotland as far north as Inverness.

Under Emperor Trajan, who preceded Hadrian, the empire had grown significantly. But there had been a number of revolts in the eastern Mediterranean, and one in Britain. When Hadrian became emperor he was concerned that the empire was over extended, and he wanted to consolidate it within a defensible border. Therefore he withdrew from areas such as modern day Iraq, and what is now Scotland.

Rome's involvement in Scotland had been entirely military. There are no remains of Roman towns or villas in Scotland, unlike in England. But there are many remains of forts and marching camps. Rome had tried to dominate the area north of the wall, but resistance had been too great, and although the Romans could almost invariably win pitched battles, the off and on guerilla warfare must have just been too costly.

Building Hadrian's Wall

Hadrian's Wall was built on the orders of the Emperor Hadrian who visited England in 122 AD. The wall represented an early border between approximately what was to become England and Scotland. However on the eastern side it is about sixty-five miles (105 km) south of the current border, reducing to a mile or so at its western end.

Before Hadrian's Wall was built the Romans had a line of forts along the Stanegate, a road between Corbridge and Carlisle. It was decided to concentrate on this area and build a wall separating Roman controlled Britain from the land of the barbarians. The wall was built up to two miles (3.2 km) north of the Stanegate, following a line that was more defensible than the line of the road. It follows a low valley created by the rivers Irthing in the west and Tyne in the east, across the narrowest route from the east to the west coast of England. In the middle of the country the wall runs along the Winn Sill, a rocky outcrop with a cliff on its north side, and therefore an excellent defensive position. However, much of the wall doesn't have the luxury of such a naturally defensive site.

There were four elements to the defensive network Hadrian instructed be built. Where there wasn't a natural defense such as a cliff, a ditch was dug in front of the wall to slow down an attack. Then there was the wall itself. Behind the wall, to allow fast communications and troop movements along the wall, the Romans built a military road. Behind the road they dug the vallum, a major ditch. The vallum was from a few hundred feet to a mile (1.6 km) south of the wall. The purpose of the vallum is unclear. Some historians believe that the area from the wall to the vallum was a militarized zone, which civilians could only enter when permitted to do so. Others believe that the Romans were concerned that some of the southern tribes might revolt, so the vallum provided an element of defense in the rear of the wall. It would also have presented a significant obstacle to raiding bands that had breached the wall returning north with their booty.

The wall is seventy-four miles (119 km) long, has fifteen forts (although there is some dispute about the precise number of forts), eighty-one milecastles (Roman miles were slightly shorter than our miles), and two turrets between each milecastles. The main garrison was stationed in the large forts which were built along the wall, such as Housesteads, or some of the original Stanegate forts slightly behind it, such as Vindolanda. The main forts were usually about five miles (8 km) apart, and when at full complement would have had a garrison of five hundred to a thousand troops. Milecastles were garrisoned with twenty to thirty solders, and each milecastle had a gate through the wall. The turrets were watchtowers, and probably held about eight men. When at full complement the wall's garrison would be about 10,000 men.

5. The Remains of a Milecastle, showing the gates through the wall.

The wall connecting the turrets was built last. The width of the eastern section of the wall to Planetrees near Chollerford is 10 Roman feet (about 3 metres). At Planetrees the width reduces to 8 Roman feet, presumably to speed up construction. However the foundations continued at 10 Roman feet, indicating that plans were changed after the foundations had been laid, and the building of the wall was proceeding in an east to west direction. In the west the wall was initially built of turf, presumably to erect a defensive structure quickly. Also stone was not readily available in the area, nor was lime for mortar. However, it was fairly quickly replaced by a stone wall. The wall ends at the village of Bowness-on-Solway, but a line of forts, milecastles and turrets continue south along the coast for 25 miles to defend against attackers from the sea.

No part of the wall remains to its original height. However, the widely held view is that the wall would have been about 15 feet (about 4.5 metres) high, with a walkway at the top and battlements to give the troops protection when attacked. At 15 feet troops on the wall would have been able to see and fire into the bottom of the ditch in front of the wall.

We know a lot about the building of the wall because of the inscribed stones the troops left to record their achievement in building it. Analysis of these proved it was built on the instructions of the emperor Hadrian, and show when it was built because of references on the stones to the provincial governor at the time.

What Was the Wall Actually For?

It is difficult to envisage that a milecastle and a turret or two, with a combined garrison of perhaps 40 men, could hold back an attack of several thousand northern tribesmen for more than five minutes. However, in times of peace the milecastle may have operated as a sort of customs post, ensuring that only goods and people approved by the Romans passed through the wall, and perhaps charging customs duty.

In times of war those parts of the wall that did not have a major fort would only be able to stop small raiding parties. But, whilst a major raiding party could almost certainly get over the wall, they would have much greater difficulty getting back when the whole of the wall's garrison had been mobilized and the raiding party was laden down with booty and driving stolen livestock. The northern tribesmen were also known for their light cavalry, and without a wall joining the forts small raiding parties could have used the cover of darkness to bypass the forts on the Stanegate and raid into northern England.

The wall would therefore have been quite a deterrent. It was also a statement of power. Some historians believe it would have originally been whitewashed. It must have astounded the local population.

The Antonine Wall

Eight years after the wall was completed Hadrian died and Antoninus Pius was appointed emperor. He needed a military conquest during his reign to increase his credibility as emperor, so he decided to instruct his generals to invade north of the wall. However, taking over all of what is now Scotland proved too costly, and therefore a new wall, the Antonine Wall, was built 100 miles (160 kilometres) north of Hadrian's Wall, between the Forth and Clyde estuaries in central Scotland. Work started in 142 AD and, although at 39 miles (63 kilometres), it is shorter than Hadrian's Wall and built largely of turf, it took about 12 years to complete. In about 162 AD, only 8 years after completion, the Antonine Wall was abandoned and Hadrian's Wall was reoccupied as the frontier defense.

In 208 the Romans again moved the frontier north to the Antonine Wall, but pulled back to Hadrian's Wall a few years later. A possible explanation for their withdrawal is that the border tribes between Hadrian's Wall and the Antonine Wall were never successfully pacified, and the Romans on the Antonine Wall found themselves with a dangerous enemy to their rear.

Visiting Hadrian's Wall

Little of Hadrian's Wall exists at the highly populated Carlisle and Newcastle ends. Actually, the stone still exists, but has been robbed and incorporated into buildings, farmsteads and field walls. Lanercost Priory and Carlisle Castle have been built with a considerable amount of wall stone

The most damaging period for the wall though was around 1750. During the 1745 Jacobite rebellion an English army was based in Newcastle on England's east coast, but was not able to get across the Pennines quickly to engage the Jacobite army when it attacked Carlisle in the west. So a decision was taken to build a cross Pennine road, now partly followed by the B6318. This was before there was any great concern for conservation, and parts of the wall were used as hardcore for the road! In the middle of the country though, in remote and high areas where fewer people live, the wall hasn't been robbed to the same extent and impressive sections of the wall, forts, milecastles and towers still exist to four or five feet in height.

It is well worth the drive south from the current border to see Hadrian's Wall. You can get to the Wall in various ways. One option is to drive down the A68 from Jedburgh, and then head west along the B6318, a drive of about forty-five miles (72 km) each way from Jedburgh. Another way of seeing the wall is by travelling in the AD122 bus, called after the year construction started on the wall. This is a hop-on, hop-off tourist bus running from Hexham to Haltwhistle, and stopping at the best sites on the middle section of the wall. There are bus or train connections from Newcastle and Carlisle to Hexham and Haltwhistle. Google AD122 bus to get the timetable and details. Bring walking boots, so you can walk along sections of the wall. Or better still, the length of the wall has been made a national walking trail, and each year many thousands of people walk the wall, usually in six or seven days. **http://www.visithadrianswall.co.uk/** is a good source of information.

Whether walking, or travelling on bus or car, the best sites are on the AD122 bus route and include:

Walltown, and the Roman Army Museum (CA8 7JB). This is the best museum on the wall, and it is sited close to the spectacular part of the wall shown in figure 1 on page 1, so both can visited at this location. The museum includes reconstructions, objects excavated along Hadrian's Wall and a film, Edge of Empire, which is in 3D. There is a trailer for the film on youtube.

6. Housesteads Fort.

Housesteads Fort (NE47 6NN), a major fort on the wall. Housesteads has a commanding position on the Winn Sill ridge. There is much to see, and the walk along the course of the wall from Housesteads is spectacular.

Chesters Fort and Museum (NE46 4EU). Chesters was usually the base of a 500 man cavalry unit. Chesters has the usual playing card shape of a Roman fort. It was built on the wall, with three of its sides projecting north of the wall, and a gate on each side. Therefore three of its gates opened onto the north side of the wall, into "barbarian" territory. This meant that the cavalry could quickly be launched to deal with any disturbances on the north side of the wall. Chesters also protected a bridge over the River Tyne, which has now largely disappeared.

Vindolanda (NE47 7JN), a fort which is just south of the wall. The greatest find at Vindolanda, of global significance, is hundreds of slim wooden writing tablets which have survived for 1900 years under the soil. The soil around Vindolanda is anaerobic, which means there is no air in it. Therefore objects in the soil do not deteriorate to the same extent they would in an aerobic soil.

First discovered in 1973, the tablets required scientific treatment before writing could be made out, and even then they were difficult to decipher because they were written in an unusual form of Latin script. Tablets are still being found and provide a unique insight into life on Rome's northern frontier. Some are on display at Vindolanda, in a new state of the art, special hermetically sealed case, protected from the decaying influence of oxygen, moisture and humidity. They have been described as like postcards from the past.

7. Two walkers on Hadrian's Wall path.

The wall deserves a whole book on its own. In fact, a series of books. I can thoroughly recommend Hadrian's Wall, by Derry Brabbs, (published by Frances Lincoln Ltd, 2008), and Hadrian's Wall, Edge of an Empire, by Ed Geldard, (The Crowood Press, 2011). Both books provide a good overview, and their photographs are stunning.

There are a range of books for people planning to walk the wall, and companies which will arrange accommodation and move baggage between your hotels or bed and breakfast accommodation. Simply googling "Hadrian's Wall Path" or visiting **http://www.visithadrianswall.co.uk/** is a good starting point.

3. THE REIVERS

Background to the Reivers

The Borders are renowned for the border reivers. They were rustlers, bandits and thieves - gangsters who caused mayhem, particularly in the 1500s and up to the union of the Scottish and English crowns in 1603. They existed on both sides of the border and often raided where pickings were best, not making a distinction between Scotland and England. They ran protection rackets; the vulnerable would often pay these gangsters in oats, barley or meal, known as blackmeal, from which the word "blackmail" derives. Their raiding parties could be small bands of a handful of men, up to small armies of more than a thousand.

Reivers rode small, agile horses, and were often armed with a lance, as in the picture. Reivers who could afford one in the 16th century carried single shot pistols known as daggs, which because of their limited accuracy were only effective at close range, and might not fire in damp weather. So even in the second half of the 16th century bows and arrows were still in widespread use.

What created the reivers? As described in chapter 1 the border area in the 14th, 15th and 16th centuries saw frequent cross border incursions by the armies of Scotland and England, laying waste to their enemy's territory and terrorising the inhabitants. The rough wooing of the 16th century, in which Henry VIII used marauding, murder and mayhem to terrorize the Scots was a continuation of this. Borderers were brought up in a climate of violence, and became desensitized to murder, rape and robbery. On both side of the border they were rightly cynical about the ability of their governments to protect them. This resulted in a self-reliant and battle-hardened population, who looked to their extended families and borderers with the same surname for support, rather than the government.

For administrative purposes the English and Scottish crowns divided the Borders into three administrative districts, called Marches, each under the control of a March Warden. Each country had a west, middle and east March. Of course, the boundaries of the English and Scottish Marches didn't coincide – that would have been too much to ask, but there was some approximation. The March Warden's duty was to police the March and dispense justice, but in practice they were often just as corrupt as the reivers they were supposed to police.

8. The reiver statue in front of Galashiels War Memorial. The statue is an accurate representation of a reiver.

There was even a strip of land called the debatable land which neither country even nominally controlled. It was about 12 miles (19.5 km) long and 3 miles (5 km) wide, and ran in a north east direction from the river

Esk north of Carlisle, almost to Langholm. England and Scotland disputed ownership of this area, and probably had for centuries. It therefore attracted outlaws and renegades from both nations, as neither England nor Scotland felt they were responsible for imposing law and order. The Grahams in particular settled here in some numbers.

In 1552 commissioners from Scotland and England finally managed, after much argument, and with the French Ambassador as referee, to divide it between the kingdoms. It is now partly in Cumbria in England and Dumfries and Galloway in Scotland, where it includes the town of Canonbie. A three mile (5 km) earth dike was constructed in an east-west direction to mark the border in the debatable land.

The Borders in the 16th century was effectively a failed state – largely ungoverned and ungovernable. The similarities with modern day Afghanistan resonate. It made the American "wild west" in the 19th century look like a kindergarten. If only there was a local film industry, the Borders would have been known throughout the world in the way Hollywood made the American west famous.

But it is wrong to think of this era and the reivers in romantic terms. This was bloody destruction, rape and pillage, not daring-do. These were not "Robin Hood" characters - they were hard men trying to survive and prosper in a hard environment, with few scruples about how they did it.

There is some evidence that the English government was not unhappy that the Borders were almost ungovernable. To have a violent and lawless area reaching to within 30 miles (48 km) of Edinburgh, the Scottish capital, weakened the Scottish government, whilst not threatening England's capital of London 300 miles (483 km) south of the border. There were even occasional reiver raids into the villages bordering Edinburgh.

The reivers often raided on their own side of the Border. However it could often be less dangerous for English reivers to raid in Scotland and Scottish reivers to raid in England, because whilst in theory the law could be enforced across the Border, in practice this often did not happen. Therefore cross-border raiders could often obtain some protection in their home country, particularly if they had what we would now call the right political connections. But they often stole from and harried their fellow countrymen - they had little concept of country in any event. So this was not a straightforward Scotland versus England matter. In kinship terms the border provided a rather artificial divide, and a Kerr or Graham in Scotland would often prefer to side with their kin in England rather than with the Scottish state. Many reivers did not see themselves as Scottish or English, and there are numerous stories of reivers changing sides in battles between Scotland and England to ensure they would be on the winning side.

The borderers were usually livestock rather than arable farmers, and their main assets were their sheep and cattle. Even on land where arable farming would have been productive, it was often not sensible as raiding armies were adept at stealing or burning crops. The borderers therefore often raised livestock, as this was moveable when raiders were in the area. Unfortunately this was also stealable. During minor raids livestock could be kept secure in the ground floor of pele towers, or in protected barmkins (walled enclosures) beside the pele. When there was notice of a major raid or incursion by an army which the pele couldn't be defended against, borderers would often move their livestock to hidden upland pastures, or into mosses or woods, hiding them from trouble.

October to March was the main time for raiding. The weather was too bad to allow livestock to graze freely on the upland pastures for long periods. Therefore the farmers gathered their cattle and sheep together in herds in the lowlands. This made it easier for the reivers to rustle a complete herd quickly and to get away. Also, the raiding party was able to use the cover of the long dark nights. October and November were particularly favored for reiving, as at the beginning of the winter the ground might be dry, rather than waterlogged, and cattle were fit enough to be driven some distance at speed, after a summer of grazing.

The main reiving families were renowned and feared in southern Scotland and northern England. In 1525 Gavin Dunbar, the Catholic Archbishop of Glasgow, when not burning Protestants (this was leading up to the Protestant reformation in Scotland in 1560), issued his famous curse in which he excommunicated the reivers. The following is an extract, updated to modern English.

"I curse their head and all the hairs of their head; I curse their face, their eye, their mouth, their nose, their tongue, their teeth, their forehead, their shoulders, their breast, their heart, their stomach, their back, their womb, their arms, their legs, their hands, their feet, and every part of their body, from the top of their head to the soles of their feet, before and behind, within and without.

I curse them going and I curse them riding; I curse them standing and I curse them sitting; I curse them eating and I curse them drinking; I curse them rising, and I curse them lying; I curse them at home, I curse them away from home; I curse them within the house, I curse them outside of the house; I curse their wives, their children, and their servants who participate in their deeds."

9. The Curse Stone.

And it goes on and on and on. For the year 2000 celebrations, Carlisle council commissioned a 14 ton granite stone with the curse inscribed, and it stands in an underpass between Carlisle Castle and the Tullie House Museum. The Archbishop should have saved his breath, as his curse had no effect. The decades after it was issued saw more reiving than ever.

The following incidents, the first of very rough justice, the second of a daring jail break, and the remainder of deadly border feuds, give a picture of what life could be like in the Borders in the 16th century.

The Hanging of Johnnie Armstrong

The story is simple. The 1520's were a lawless time in the Borders. The English authorities were increasingly incensed by Scottish raids and threatening to take things into their own hands in Scotland. James V knew he had to do something to assert his authority over the Scottish Borders, or risk England's Henry VIII doing it. He started in 1530 by summoning the Border Earls and chiefs to Edinburgh, including Scott of Buccleuch, Bothwell, Douglas of Drumlanrig, Hume, Johnstone and Maxwell, and locked them up for failing to keep order and in many cases being involved in thievery themselves. He wanted to show them who was in charge.

Johnnie (also known as Black Jock) Armstrong was a well-known reiver and, whilst a very colorful individual, not a nice man. He didn't go to Edinburgh, but he and a band of about 35 of his followers were enticed, possibly with a safe conduct, to meet the king who had taken a large force of possibly 10,000 men into the Armstrong's heartland of Liddesdale. However, rather than be treated as honored guests as they expected, the Armstrong band found themselves surrounded by King James's soldiers.

Instead of taking the band back to Edinburgh for a trial and then hanging them (for most of them deserved hanging many times over), King James had them hung on the spot. It may be that the young king was annoyed by the Armstrong's wealth and cockiness. King James V of Scotland was only seventeen at the time, and like many teenage boys with testosterone surging through their veins, likely to be impulsive and easy to anger.

A famous Borders ballad has Johnnie Armstrong addressing the king when he recognized the game was up:

> "To seek het water beneath cauld ice,
> Surely it is a great folie –
> I have asked grace at a graceless face,
> But there is nane for my men and me"

This extract comes from a ballad, not a contemporaneous account of the incident. However it may give at least a flavor of the incident.

There is a memorial near Carlenrig church, where the incident took place. The King's action may have been severe, but its effect on law and order in the Borders was only temporary. In a few years the Borders returned to disorder.

Kinmont Willie and His Escape from Carlisle Castle

Another major incident in the history of the Armstrong clan was the escape of Kinmont Willie Armstrong from Carlisle Castle in 1596. Kinmont Willie, a well-known reiver, was captured by the English Warden of the West March on a truce day. Truce days were often held several times a year, when the English and Scots Wardens would meet to settle cross-border disputes. Those attending the meeting were entitled to safe conduct. The immunity of truce days made negotiation possible, and the settling of at least some disputes without bloodshed. Kinmont Willie deserved to be arrested, but arresting him on a truce day was illegal.

Willie was imprisoned in Carlisle Castle, one of the border's most impregnable strongholds, and described on pages 29 to 30. The Warden of the Scottish West March, Scott of Buccleuch, first tried diplomacy to get Willie set free, writing to everyone of note, including the English ambassador to the Scottish court. When this proved ineffective it was time to take more direct measures. The arrest had offended the whole reiver community and for once they decided to act together. The strength of Carlisle Castle did not daunt Willie's allies. However, although they could easily have mustered several thousand riders, they did not have the equipment and experience for a frontal attack on a major castle. Also this would have amounted to an act of war, with potentially catastrophic consequences. Stealth was the answer.

The 13 April 1596 was a dark and rainy night – the sort of night when anyone who could stay indoors did so, and therefore the reivers were less likely to be spotted. A party of 80 reivers (Armstrongs, Elliots, Scotts, Bells and Grahams) rode under cover of darkness to the walls of the castle. They knew Willie was being held in a house in the lower courtyard of the castle, near an old postern gate (a small secondary gate, not the main gate into the castle).

The gang may have bribed the guards, or have gained entry to the gate by removing the stones surrounding the door bolt. Reivers were adept at this – they often forced entry to farms and pele towers in this way. They then moved quietly to the house within the castle compound in which the old reiver was imprisoned. They released him and made their escape into the dark and rain swept night. It is likely that as well as bribing the guards to look the other way, they had prepared ambushes at strategic points on their escape route to disrupt any following party of troops from the castle. This was a standard reiver tactic. However it wasn't necessary – no one dared to follow them into the dark night.

The incident caused a diplomatic furor all the way up to Queen Elizabeth I, and eventually Buccleuch was required by James VI, because of diplomatic pressure from Elizabeth, to go to Elizabeth and apologize. Apparently Elizabeth was impressed by Buccleuch, and is reported to have said *"With ten thousand such men, our brother in Scotland might shake the firmest throne of Europe"*.

The Carlisle raid was one of the last great episodes in reiving history – only seven years later Elizabeth was dead, to be replaced by King James of Scotland. This changed the whole dynamics of the Anglo-Scottish border. James was determined to stamp out reiving, and did this effectively.

Two Great Reiver Feuds

There were many feuds between the border clans, but two in particular were long and bloody.

Scott and Kerr Feud

From 1525 to 1528 the young James V of Scotland was held "under the protection" of his step-father Archibald Douglas, Earl of Angus. He was virtually the Earl's prisoner, which allowed the Earl to assume the authority of the king, on the pretense he was implementing the king's will. However, the young king managed to get a message to Sir Walter Scott, (not the famous author, who wasn't born for another 250 years), asking for his help.

In July 1526 King James was being escorted to Edinburgh by Douglas supported by a large body of Kerrs, when the party was intercepted by a force of Scotts and Elliots led by Sir Walter. The fighting was hard in what became known as the battle of Melrose, but turned against Scott when Lord Hume arrive with 80 Kerrs and charged into Scott's left wing. The Scott and Elliot forces retreated, but during the ensuing chase Andrew Kerr of Cessford was killed (by an Elliot actually, not a Scott). However the incident resulted in a long blood feud between the Scotts and the Kerrs.

There were various attempts to heal the blood feud, such as the marriage of Sir Walter Scott of Buccleuch to a Kerr. However, over two decades later resentment was still smoldering, and in 1552 Sir Walter Scott of Buccleuch was finally knifed to death by a gang of Kerrs whilst he was walking in the High Street of Edinburgh. This led to more bad blood and retaliation, but the feud was eventually ended by treaties and further marriages between the families.

Johnstone and Maxwell Feud

The feud between the Johnstones and Maxwells went on for over a century. Its origins are lost in history, but it was kept alive by rivalry for the wardenship of the West March. The Maxwells and their supporters had the greatest military muscle and so Maxwell was the more dominant clan, and therefore the clan head was the obvious choice as warden. In practice the wardenship sometimes changed hands between Maxwells and Johnstones. Whenever it changed hands, it was just putting a different fox in charge of the henhouse.

However the Maxwell clan was compromised in the mind of James VI because it remained Catholic long after Scotland became Protestant in 1560. In 1585 the king instructed Johnstone, who was warden, to arrest Lord Maxwell because of his Catholic beliefs. The king then had to backtrack and accept Maxwell as warden because the Maxwells went on the rampage, destroying Johnstone property and holding the Johnstone warden prisoner.

It was to the advantage of England that the feud continued, as they then faced a disunited Scottish force in the West March, so the English warden sometimes intervened on one side or the other when it suited English policy.

The feud reached its height in 1593. A Johnstone reiver stole a horse belonging to the Crichtons who lived in upper Nithsdale. He was pursued by a band of Crichtons, who caught and hung him. The Johnstones swore revenge for the death of their kinsman, and so in response a party of Johnstones carried out a raid in Crichton territory. Maxwell entered into an agreement with the Crichtons and Douglases to combine against the Johnstones. A copy of the agreement fell into the hands of the leader of the Johnstone clan, putting him on his guard. When Maxwell did eventually act Johnstone was prepared.

Maxwell formed a small army of about 2000 for his raid against the Johnstones. The Johnstones had less than half that force at their disposal. However the Laird of Johnstone was a wily adversary. When the Maxwell force advanced, the Johnstones and their allies ambushed them on 6 December 1593 at Dryfe Sands. This is on the river Dryfe near Lockerbie, later famous as the town where Pan Am flight 103 crashed to earth after a bomb exploded on board. The Johnstone force surprised the Maxwell vanguard, and pushed it back into the main force, breaking the main body up in confusion. After hard and confused fighting the Johnstones killed Lord Maxwell and won the day.

That did not end the feud however. In 1608, five years after the union of the Scottish and English crowns, the then Lord Maxwell (the son of the Lord Maxwell who died at Dryfe Sands) and James Johnstone met. They were only accompanied by a servant apiece, the private meeting having been arranged to discuss putting a final end to the dispute. However Maxwell's solution was far-reaching – he shot James Johnstone twice in the back, killing him. Maxwell then escaped to the continent, but eventually returned to Scotland, only to be betrayed by a relative, the Earl of Caithness. By now law and order was in the ascendant, and Lord Maxwell was hanged for murder.

The above is only an overview of this terrible but fascinating time. For a more in-depth coverage I recommend "The Steel Bonnets" by George Macdonald Fraser, and "The Reivers: the Story of the Border Reivers" by Alistair Moffat.

4. BORDER FORTIFICATIONS

Major Castles on the Scottish Side

There are fewer large scale castles in the Scottish Borders than the Welsh Borders. There are several reasons for this. Unlike in Wales, where Edward 1 built many magnificent, state-of-the-art castles, Edward had to take a different approach in Scotland. He had run out of money by the time he invaded Scotland, and couldn't afford a big building project.

Some of the most important Scottish fortifications such as Roxburgh and Jedburgh, which were built before long-term hostilities began, were destroyed - not by the English, but by the Scots. Because of the significant mismatch in military resources, the Scots were much more effective at guerrilla tactics than in holding static defensive positions. When major castles were taken by English armies, they were used by the invaders as a centre for dominating the surrounding countryside. So when the Scots retook the castle, knowing that it would probably be retaken in the next major invasion by the English army, the Scots slighted the castle (that is they knocked key elements down, to render it indefensible). Over succeeding centuries the locals then used the stone for building materials, so little remains of Roxburgh Castle for example. The Scottish side of the border makes up for its scarcity of major castles by its many small tower houses.

Even so, there are still some imposing castles in the Scottish Borders. Let us look at five of the main ones.

Threave Castle
Near Postcode DG7 1TJ

10. Threave Castle on its island in the River Dee.

Threave Castle was a mighty Douglas stronghold on the far west of the Borders, close to the town of Castle Douglas. Threave is built on an island in the middle of the River Dee, accessible by a ferry or in the past by a hidden causeway. Visitors should be aware it is a 10 to 15 minute walk from the car park.

The island has probably been used as a defensive stronghold from the year dot, but the tower that dominates it today was built for Archibald Douglas, the Lord of Galloway, in the late 1300s. At the time Douglas needed a strong castle because of the danger of attack from his two main enemies, the Gallovidians (the people of Galloway, of whom he was notionally the Lord), and the English.

At its peak, the island on which the castle stands would also have had a whole range of buildings for retainers, and workshops for craftsmen providing services to support their Lord's household.

The castle had several layers of defense. The River Dee itself provided a major hurdle for attackers – in the Middle Ages it would have been far wider than today's channeled river, and many of the fields on its banks would have been marshland. Secondly, there was a ditch around the tower. Thirdly in about 1447, (the date was confirmed by tree-ring dating of timber gateposts and coin finds), a low level artillery wall was built round the tower-house, to provide protection from an enemy's artillery. This state of the art artillery defense included three towers where the defenders could mount their artillery. And finally, the immensely strong tower-house itself.

King James II, having grown concerned about the Black Douglases' increasing wealth and power, decided to bring them to heal. He murdered the Earl of Douglas at Stirling Castle in 1452. The Black Douglases' power came to the end in 1455, when King James set about systematically destroying the Douglas castles, Threave being the last on his list. When the new Douglas clan head was abroad in France the castle withstood a siege of two months, and only capitulated when the garrison was bribed by the king. King James, like kings do, then took ownership of the castle.

11. Threave Castle in close-up, showing the low artillery fortification in front of the tower.

In the 1500s the castle was acquired by the Maxwells. This was ultimately to lead to its downfall. Its last great siege was in 1640 during what is known as the Bishops' Wars, in which the Maxwell owner of Threave and of Caerlaverock, a great Borders' castle we will discuss next, supported King Charles I against the Covenanters. Charles was trying to impose an Anglican style of worship, and a governance structure including bishops, on the church in Scotland. The Covenanters strongly supported the Presbyterian form of church governance and an extreme form of the Protestant religion. As described in chapter 1 the fiercely independent Scots wanted to appoint their own church ministers, rather than have bishops controlling the appointment and controlling church affairs. Under the Anglican form of church governance as was in place in England the bishops would have reported to the king as head of the church. As the Maxwell family were Catholic adherents for decades after Scotland became Protestant, they were predisposed to Charles's views on worship and governance.

The Covenanters, under Lieutenant Colonel Hume (another prominent Border family), laid siege to the castle for 13 weeks, until Charles I authorized it to surrender. It then was slighted by the Covenanters.

Whilst in the area, a short detour will take you to Orchardton Tower, built by the Cairns family (near postcode DG7 1QH). Orchardton is the only round tower house in Scotland, although there are many in Ireland. The builder may well have come from Ireland – then as now there would have been a great deal of contact between Dumfries and Galloway and Ireland.

The tower house is in fact quite narrow, and much of the accommodation would have been in an attached building that now only exists in a few layers of stone above ground.

Caerlaverock Castle

Postcode DG1 4RU

Caerlaverock is one of the most attractive castle ruins in the UK. It is a moated, triangular castle, eight miles (13 km) south east of Dumfries. The Maxwell family built it around 1277, and until 1640 it was their principle seat.

12. Caerlaverock Castle.

It is the only three sided castle in Britain. It has a circular tower on both corners of its south wall, and its east and west walls come together in a twin towered gatehouse at the north end of the castle. The current castle was built in the 1270s and replaced a castle built about fifty years earlier on a site 220 yards (200 metres) closer to the Solway Firth. The earlier castle possibly proved unstable and subject to flooding as it was built in a marshy area. More recently archaeologists have discovered the remains of an even earlier fortification on the site of the old castle, so the area would have been fortified for several hundred years before 1270.

Sited close to the border, Caerlaverock saw a great deal of action in the English-Scottish wars. The first major siege was in 1300 when an English army of over 3000, commanded by Edward I, was delayed for 2 days by the 60 defenders of the castle, before the defenders capitulated.

Caerlaverock was besieged five times from 1270, and changed hands between England and Scotland several times. The last great siege was in 1640. As its Maxwell owners supported Charles I in the Bishops' Wars, the Covenanters besieged it at the same time as they were attacking Threave. The castle was damaged during the thirteen week siege, and eventually had to capitulate. After the castle surrendered to the Covenanters it was slighted by knocking down much of the south wall, so it couldn't be used for defense in future. After that it was abandoned, and became a romantic ruin, much painted by artists. In 1634, only six years before the siege, the Maxwells had spent a fortune building a small palace called the Nithsdale Lodgings inside the walls. How is that for bad timing!

The castle is attractive and moated – a great place to visit with children. It is now in the capable hands of Historic Scotland, and has a range of displays about siege warfare and weapons that should interest younger as well as older visitors. The grounds lead to nature trails in the adjoining woodland.

Hermitage Castle
Postcode TD9 0LU

13. Hermitage Castle, grim and formidable.

Hermitage Castle stands grim, formidable and brooding, radiating power. Strangely though it was also involved in one of Scotland's most famous love affairs. It is sited twelve miles (20 km) south of Hawick in the Hermitage Valley just off Liddesdale, covering one of the main routes into Scotland in medieval times. Liddesdale was the most lawless valley in the Borders, which is really saying something. Hermitage provided protection for anyone trying to police this dangerous place.

The U.K. has a horrible history series of books aimed at teaching history to children by focusing on the more gory aspects – a whole book could have been dedicated to Hermitage. Hermitage is not a picture-postcard castle; it was designed for war, and saw plenty of it. The first castle on the site, a simple motte and bailey castle, was built in about 1240, and was involved in the Wars of Independence. In 1338, it was in the hands of an Englishman, Sir Ralph de Neville. It was attacked and taken for Scotland by Sir William Douglas.

The Douglases added four massive towers to the original towerhouse, one in each corner. Like many castles Hermitage had provision for a wooden fighting platform which jutted out from the walls and could be erected when needed. To allow the fighting platform to cross between the towers, arches were built between the towers on the east and west sides. The openings along the top of the walls, which today could be mistaken as windows are in fact doors, so troops could enter the fighting platform. The row of square holes below the line of doors are to anchor supports for the platform.

As well as a moat, the castle was protected by a small river, Hermitage Water, and a large area of marsh, making attack difficult. Once attackers had got though the marsh and over the moat, for several centuries the main entrance was at first floor level. The wooden stairway to the first floor would of course have been removed by the defenders when an attack was expected. However, assuming the attackers managed to get up to and through the wooden door, the defenders then had a pretty nasty trick up their sleeves. The attackers would see a portcullis before them. However, when they reached this portcullis the defenders would lower a second portcullis **behind** the attackers, trapping them in a "killing zone", where they could be finished off with boiling liquid which penetrated their armour, or arrows fired through murder holes.

There are many legends surrounding Hermitage. One is that the first owner of a castle on the site, de Soulis, was in league with the devil. He had a pact with the devil that he could not be killed by iron or rope, and so he could not be killed by a weapon or by hanging. The borderers were nothing if not ingenious though – the legend is that they boiled him alive!

An early owner, Sir William Douglas, committed one of the black acts of the castle. Jealous of Sir Alexander Ramsay, who had been appointed by the King as Sheriff of Teviotdale, he kidnapped Sir Alexander, imprisoned him in Hermitage and starved him to death. Sir William was not a man to fall out with. When Sir William died, the castle passed to his son James Douglas, later to be the hero of the battle of Otterburn, and then to George Douglas, the illegitimate son of Sir William. George became the first Earl of Angus and founder of the Red Douglas line, so called because of his red hair.

By the 1490s Archibald Douglas, the owner of Hermitage, was getting too close to the English for the liking of the Scottish king, James IV. Hermitage was near the border and so it was strategically important. Therefore James IV required Archibald to exchange Hermitage for Bothwell Castle, then controlled by the Earl of Bothwell. Bothwell Castle was less strategic as it was in Lanarkshire, much further from the border.

During the fourth Earl of Bothwell's tenure at Hermitage their occurred one of the castle's most famous incidents. In 1566 James Hepburn, the fourth Earl, was injured in a skirmish with a reiver, Wee Jock Elliot, and was taken to Hermitage. Mary, Queen of Scots, who had been linked romantically with Bothwell, was in Jedburgh about 25 miles (40 km) away, on a royal tour of the Borders. When Mary heard of Bothwell's injury, she immediately made the 25 mile journey with a small party to Hermitage to see him. After two hours with Bothwell, she rode back the 25 miles to Jedburgh. Perhaps she had pressing business in Jedburgh, or considered it inappropriate to spend the night in the castle. These would have been very difficult and exposed journeys across bleak moorland in October. On the return journey her horse threw her at one point. When back in Jedburgh she was ill with a fever that nearly killed her.

Cessford Castle
Postcode TD5 8EG

14. Cessford Castle.

Cessford Castle is now quite ruinous, but was a very strong and large-scale castle, with major outworks that no longer exist. It belonged to the Cessford branch of the Kerr family. The Kerrs were a major reiving family and sometime Warden of the Middle March. They were one of the most notorious gangster families in the area, and needed a strong castle to protect them from their enemies. With walls of thirteen feet (four metres) thick for the main tower, a curtain wall and a moat, it was certainly strong.

The castle is situated close to the border and about 6 miles (9 km) from the A68 road, which run along what was a major invasion route into Scotland. But is wasn't just English incursions the Kerrs needed protection against. They were often in conflict with the Kerrs of Ferniehirst Castle, and had a long running and bloody feud with the Scotts.

Cessford was the site of numerous sieges, including in 1523 when the Earl of Surrey besieged the castle in the absence of the owner, Sir Andrew Ker (he spelt his name Ker, not the now common Kerr). The attackers managed to get over the curtain wall using scaling ladders, but were unable to gain entry to the castle. However their artillery managed to open and widen a blocked up window six feet above ground level, and their plan was to get barrels of gunpowder into the castle via the window. But the defenders managed to set off the powder before the attackers could do so, injuring a number of the attackers. The owner, Sir Andrew

Ker, returned and surrendered the castle when it was agreed he could leave with the defenders and his possessions.

The castle was again taken and burnt by the English during the rough wooing in the 1540s.

Hume Castle
Postcode TD5 7TR

15. Hume Castle. It dominates the area.

Hume Castle is situated about 25 miles (40 km) inland from Berwick overlooking the small village of Hume. It was the main castle of the Hume/Home family. The clan name is pronounced Hume, but many members retain the original spelling of Home. The Hume/Home family was the leading power in the Scottish East March. Their chief was often made March Warden by the king.

The castle is a medieval ruin within a folly. The ramparts you now see with their extravagant crenulations were built around 1770 for decorative, rather than military purposes, by the 3rd Lord Marchmont, a member of the Home family. The ramparts are approximately on the line of the exterior wall of the original castle, and inside the walls there are the remains of the original castle.

The castle stands in a dominant position in the East March, overlooking much of the March, less than 5 miles (8 km) from the English border. Therefore it was heavily involved in border warfare. The castle was immensely strong against medieval armaments and dominated the area. However it was surrender to the English invaders in 1547 when they threatened to execute Alexander Home, Lord Home's eldest son, who had been captured just before the battle of Pinkie Cleugh. However Alexander Home got his revenge when he recovered the castle in a daring night attack in December 1548, helped by spies inside the castle. The English took the castle again in 1569, and held it for five years.

By the 1600s artillery was no longer new, and had developed to such an extent to be a real threat to essentially medieval castles such as Hume. Because of its weakness against the latest artillery, the castle was doomed when in 1651 it was bombarded by Cromwell's Parliamentary army. The defenders surrendered and were allowed to leave, and then Cromwell's troops finished the job by destroying the castle with explosives.

The view of the surrounding countryside from the castle site is magnificent, and by itself more than rewards the visit.

Major Castles on the English Side

Carlisle Castle

Postcode CA3 8U

16. Carlisle Castle.

Whilst Hermitage Castle is grim and foreboding, and Caerlaverock attractive, Carlisle Castle is squat and business like. Carlisle, near the west coast, and Berwick-upon-Tweed on the east coast, were the two main military fortifications on the English side of the border in the 16th century. Carlisle, just 10 miles (16 km) from the Scottish border, was at that time a walled city with a massive and strong castle. Carlisle has been an important military centre since the time of the Romans, and probably before. Positioned at the meeting point of three rivers, the main west coast road to Scotland, and the road from the northwest of England to Newcastle, it is in a strategic position.

The castle is on the northern edge of the old town and on slightly higher ground than the town. The town walls connected to the castle, which created a strong defensive system, with the castle able to stand on its own if the town was taken.

As outlined in chapter 1, Carlisle and much of northern England was for many years disputed territory between the English and Scots. In 1066, when William the Conqueror won his victory at the Battle of Hastings, Cumberland and Carlisle were controlled by a chieftain who owed allegiance to the King of Scots. However, in 1092 William the Conqueror's son Rufus invaded the area and annexed Cumbia, including Carlisle, for England. The Normans were great castle builders, and for speed of construction he immediately began building a wooden castle. For greater security this was rebuilt in stone in 1112.

17. The Captain's Tower with the Half-Moon artillery battery below it. The ground in front of the battery used to be lower.

The castle has been added to over the centuries. The visitor or invader now goes through a strong gatehouse to enter a large outer ward. Once in the outer ward, there is a further gatehouse, called the Captains Tower, which controls access to the inner ward, the centre of the castle. In front of and below the Captain's Tower is the Half Moon battery, a semi-circular artillery fortification built in the 1540s to provide additional firepower to control access to the inner ward. In more recent times the ground level in the outer ward was raised to create a parade ground. Before that was done the Half Moon battery's field of fire allowed it to control the outer ward, if invaders had reached that far. Even that was not considered strong enough to defend against the Scots. At one time there was a moat and drawbridge in front of the Captain's Tower and Half Moon battery, to further protect access to the castle's inner ward. Within the inner ward is the castle's keep, the centre of the castle and its last redoubt.

The Scots took Carlisle in 1135 and controlled it until they withdrew in 1157 because they recognized they would be unable to hold it against an English attack. The Scots captured the castle again for a short time in 1216. However ninety nine years later in 1315, a year after the Scots major victory at Bannockburn, even Robert the Bruce was unable to capture the castle during an eleven day assault.

Around 1541, because of increased concern about an attack from the Scots in alliance with France, the castle's and town's defenses were modernized on the orders of Henry VIII. This involved strengthening some walls to withstand artillery bombardment and to enable them to carry heavy artillery. At the same time the Half-Moon gun battery was built below the Captain's Tower, to help control access to the inner ward. The inner ward's keep was lowered and its roof strengthened to take heavy guns.

During the time of the border reivers, the castle was the centre of power in the English West March, and used as a prison for border reivers. Chapter 3, The Reivers, tells of the escape of Kinmont Willie Armstrong, a particularly nefarious reiver, from captivity in the castle. Another famous prisoner was Mary, Queen of Scots, who fled to England in May 1567 following what was effectively a civil war with her Protestant subjects. She was held in the castle for several weeks when she arrived in England by boat after her flight from Scotland across the Solway Firth.

The castle's last hurrah was in 1745, during the Jacobite rebellion. Bonnie Prince Charlie and his Jacobite army made its way into England via Carlisle, and the town and castle surrendered to them. When the Jacobites retreated via Carlisle, they left a garrison of 400 men to delay the English army's pursuit. However the castle, which was designed to resist attacks made with the military hardware of the 1500s, proved no match for the artillery available in the 1700s, and after a few days of bombardment it surrendered.

The castle we see now was remodeled a little in the 1820s as a military barracks, but very extensive parts of the earlier castle remain. It is now under the protection of English Heritage.

Whilst in Carlisle it is worth visiting the cathedral, England's second smallest cathedral (postcode CA3 8TZ). The cathedral's long history goes back to the 1100s, and it is situated in its own precinct. The precinct has an attractive gatehouse, and a building called the Fratry, which was the dining hall for the monks, and is now partly used as a restaurant.

Norham Castle
Postcode TD15 2JY

This is how Sir Walter Scott described Norham in Marmion, his epic poem:

> The battled towers, the donjon keep,
> The loophole grates, where captives weep,
> The flanking walls that round it sweep,
> In yellow lustre shone.
> The warriors on the turrets high,
> Moving athwart the evening sky,
> Seem'd forms of giant height:
> Their armour, as it caught the rays,
> Flash'd back again the western blaze,
> In lines of dazzling light.

18. Norham Castle keep, through the remains of the gatehouse.

Norham is on the Tweed about 6 miles (10 km) west of Berwick-upon-Tweed, guarding what was an important ford across the river, but which has now been replaced by a bridge. The castle was built in the 1120s on the orders of the Bishop of Durham, as his Bishopric had major landholdings in the area. The castle was intended to protect against raids by the Scots.

Norham was besieged thirteen times by the Scots, and earned the reputation of being the most dangerous place in England. Inspired by their success at Bannockburn, the years after 1314 saw many Scottish incursions into Northumberland. In 1318 the Scots, under Robert the Bruce, besieged it for a year and managed to take part of the castle, but were driven out after three days. In 1319 the Scots had another try, but the castle was able to withstand a siege of seven months. In 1327 the Scots finally captured Norham, but it was restored to England when peace was declared at the Treaty of Edinburgh in 1328.

In 1513 the castle couldn't withstand Scottish artillery, and after a bombardment had to surrender to James IV. It did James little good though. A few weeks later James was killed and his army routed at the battle of Flodden.

Much of the outer works of the castle have been largely destroyed, but its huge rectangular keep remains as a ruin and demonstrates the power of the castle at its peak. Norham is an attractive ruin, and was one of a number of Northumbrian castles painted by Turner in about 1798.

Just opposite Norham, on the Scottish side of the Border, the church of Ladykirk was built in about 1500 on the orders of James IV of Scotland. It is a fortified church, with murder holes in the tower vault. As well as serving as a church, it is likely that it served as a Scottish watchtower when needed, observing Norham Castle and the ford across the Tweed.

Berwick-upon-Tweed

TD15 1NA

Berwick-upon-Tweed is now an English town on the Scottish border, although it is on the north bank (otherwise the Scottish side) of the River Tweed. It is on the main east coast rail line between London and Edinburgh, and so has an excellent rail service to the Scottish and English capitals.

The Scots took control of Berwick from the Anglo-Saxon kingdom of Northumbria in 1018, when a combined army from Scotland and Strathclyde (then separate kingdoms), defeated the Anglo-Saxons at the battle of Carham, near Coldstream on the Scottish/English border. Berwick was first captured by the English in 1296 when, in what amounted to a war crime, Edward 1's army massacred most of the population and many foreign merchants who were trading in the town. In 1318 it was retaken for Scotland by Robert the Bruce. Over the next 164 years it changed hands many times, until in 1482 the Scots gave up the contest for Berwick and it became a permanent part of England.

In such a strategic location, the town had to be heavily fortified. The defenses were built and rebuilt as the perceived threat and the latest military thinking justified. Unfortunately for history buffs the medieval castle was largely demolished for building materials, and the railway station now stands on its site. The railway platform stands on what was the castle's great hall, where in 1292 Edward I crowned John Balliol as King of Scotland. Edward intended Balliol to be a King of Scots subservient to the King of England.

Berwick-upon-Tweed has the most impressive Elizabethan fortifications of any town in the UK. These

19. An artillery emplacement in a bastion at Berwick. Designed to kill any attackers who made it to the foot of the walls.

fortifications were built between 1558 and 1570 on the orders of Mary I of England, and then her successor Elizabeth I. In 1558 Calais, England's last possession in France, had been taken by the French, and the French were encouraging the Scots to invade England. Therefore a Scottish invasion was considered a real danger. The two land-facing walls of the town were designed to incorporate the latest military thinking. Artillery was then fairly well developed, so the main element of the fortifications are very thick, relatively low walls which made a good platform for guns, and could also withstand the enemy's artillery. Protruding from the walls are five bastions. These are projecting towers intended as gun emplacements, which can allow guns to fire both forwards and along the outside of the walls, to kill any attackers who reach the walls.

To keep costs down the medieval walls were updated and reused on the less vulnerable sides facing the Tweed and the sea. The Elizabethan defenses were never used, as in 1603 the union of the crowns took place, making an Anglo-Scottish war less likely. In the subsequent Jacobite invasions of 1715 and 1745, the invading armies took the west, rather than the east coast route.

Berwick-upon-Tweed's legal status is unique, as in 1551 Edward IV made Berwick a free town independent of England and Scotland. However this is largely ignored and it is treated as a part of England. But because it is so close to Scotland and far from the heartland of England, the local football team plays in the Scottish, rather than the English, football league.

A little further south of the border on the English side are the enormous castles of Bamburgh (postcode NE69 7DF), Alnwick (postcode NE66 1NQ) and Dunstanburgh (NE66 3TT), all well worth a visit.

Pele (or Peel) Towers

The Borders is famous for its small pele towers and bastle farmhouses – a far higher number exist in the Borders than in any other part of the country.

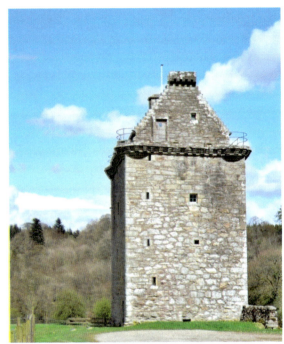
*20. Johnnie Armstrong's Tower of Gilnockie.
Postcode DG14 0XD*

Border magnates usually had their own pele tower, a fortified residence designed for living in and for defense. These were three or four stories tall, with thick stone walls. They would have provision for a lookout to stand guard on the roof, and often a beacon which could be lit to warn neighbors and summon help if the tower was threatened.

The only entrance was a door either on the ground floor, or sited above the ground floor and accessible by a removable ladder to provide an extra deterrent to the attacker. The entrance was usually protected by a thick wooden door with an iron yett behind it. The yett is an iron grill like a portcullis, and is common in fortified houses in Scotland, with a few being found in northern England. But whilst a portcullis is raised and lowered vertically, a yett opens like a door. A good example of a yett can be seen at Greenknowe Tower, less than a mile (1 km) west of the village of Gordon on the A6105 Earlston road. The tower is under the care of Historic Scotland.

Many towers had a courtyard called a barmkin attached, protected by a wall of over 6 feet (about two metres) in height. The barmkin provided an enclosed and protected area with accommodation for farm workers and room for some livestock. The barmkin could be defended against minor attacks, but in a major attack everyone would have to retreat to the much more defensible tower.

Towers were dark places, with small windows and arrow slits for defense. The external and internal doorways were often below normal height, deliberately built so that an attacker would have to slow down and stoop a little to get through.

Livestock could be protected in the ground floor of the tower during an attack. In "The Reivers: the Story of the Border Reivers" Alistair Moffat estimates that ground floors in peles are usually around 10 metres by 13 metres (about 33 by 43 feet), and that perhaps as many as 40 of the owners best cows and ponies could be protected in the ground floor during an attack. (Cows were much smaller in the 16th century than today).

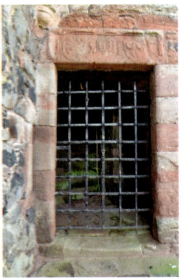
21. The Yett at Greenknowe Tower.

Smailholm Tower
Near postcode TD5 7PG

The most perfect example of a pele which is open to visitors is Smailholm tower. Smailholm's photograph appears on the front cover of this book. Smailholm is in a beautiful but rather bleak location on a rocky outcrop, giving it an excellent all round view of the area, and of any approaching danger. It is the most photographed pele tower in Scotland, and probably the fourth most photographed Scottish fortification (after Edinburgh, Stirling and Eilean Donan castles). Smailholm, which is 5 miles (8 km) northwest of Kelso, was originally owned by the Pringle family and then the Scotts, but is now under the care of Historic Scotland and open to visitors. It has strong associations with Sir Walter Scott, the author, whose grandfather at one time owned the tower and nearby farm. Scott spent some of his boyhood in nearby Sandyknowe Farm, and fell in love with the Borders.

Attacking a Pele Tower

Assuming the attackers did not have artillery, there were three usual methods of attack.

One was by stealth, and that is how the Johnstones' Lochwood Tower was taken by Sir Thomas Carleton. Carleton was Deputy Warden of the English West March, and like many officials used his position for personal enrichment. In March 1548 Carleton was reiving with a large force under his command in Dumfriesshire, and decided to take Lochwood to use as a base for his nefarious deeds.

"The Steel Bonnets" by George MacDonald Fraser has a good description of how Lockwood was taken. In summary, taking a small group of men, Carleton's party crept up to the barmkin wall in the twilight of the late March afternoon. When it was dark they climbed over the barmkin wall, and quietly took several female servants in the barmkin prisoner.

Carleton knew the tower was very lightly manned, but even so the tower would have been very difficult to take by direct assault, and without heavy weapons. Therefore he waited quietly until dawn, hiding in the barmkin with their terrified prisoners. At dawn, a female servant in the tower opened the door to go out into the barmkin. The attackers knew their moment had come, and rushed the door, managing to reach it before the servant could completely shut it. The attackers were then in, the occupants were surprised and it was all over. There were only two defenders in the tower, but even so the tower was so strongly built they could have defended it for some time if they had not been taken by surprise.

The second method of attack was to set fire to the door and other parts of the ground floor, and to smoke the defenders out. To make this more difficult the ground floor of peles often had a stone vaulted ceiling, rather than wood.

The third method of attack was to get onto the roof, and to gain entry by removing slates. This would obviously be difficult if the tower was four stories high, but was a viable strategy for smaller buildings.

Pele towers could provide excellent defense against a lightly-armed raiding party. However if the attackers were in real force, and particularly if they had artillery, the occupants would retire to the hills or disappear into the forests or mosses with their cattle and other moveable possessions.

Bastles

Another kind of defensive homestead is called a bastle (probably from the old French word bastile for fortress). Although some were in Scotland, bastles were more common on the English side of the border.

The bastle was usually a two story dwelling with thick stone walls and slits for windows. It had what was effectively a barn for livestock on the ground floor, and the farmer and his family's living quarters on the upper floor. Like pele towers, the ground floor barn often had a stone vaulted ceiling, so that any attackers who gained entry couldn't set it on fire. The barn area would have an easily defensible trapdoor to living quarters above, accessible by a removable ladder. However, the main entrance to the living quarters was by a wooden ladder on the outside wall of the bastle, to a door on the upper floor. The ladder could be pulled inside when necessary to make a successful attack more difficult.

Although usually not as defensible as a pele tower, a bastle was effective against a minor raid. The bastle had to protect its occupants for a long winter night, until help could come in the morning.

One of the best examples of a bastle house is Black Middens Bastle in Northumberland. It doesn't seem to have a postcode, but it is about 200 yards (180 metres) north of a minor road, 7 miles (11 km) north-west of Bellingham (postcode NE48 2DG), or along a minor road from the A68. It is now under the care of English Heritage. And if you study old barns and farm buildings in the north of England carefully, it is clear that many were originally built as bastle houses. There is even an Armstrong bastle within the boundaries of Housesteads fort on Hadrian's Wall, built of stone robbed from the fort of course. (Housesteads is some distance from key Armstrong territory around Liddesdale. Perhaps this Armstrong didn't get on with the rest!)

Fortified Ecclesiastical Buildings

22. Newton Arlosh church. When reivers were in the area, the tower provided protection for the villagers.

The major abbeys, monasteries and many churches had a degree of fortification. It might be thought that in a highly Christian time these religious buildings would be considered immune from battle. However, in times of war they were used as mustering points and supply depots for armies, which put them in the military front line. They also might have wealth, making them a very attractive target. And lastly, in the 16th century for about 35 years England was Protestant whilst Scotland was Catholic, and at that time raiders thought they had "carte blanche" to pillage and destroy religious houses if they worshipped another version of Christianity.

One of the best preserved fortified churches is St John the Baptist at Newton Arlosh (approximate postcode CA7 5ET), a small village to the west of Carlisle in Cumbria. It now seems a distance from the Borders, but the reivers were adept at crossing the Solway Firth at fording points which were available at low tide. Other English examples include Kirknewton and Ancroft. Ladykirk on the Tweed is a Scottish example (see Norham Castle for more details of Ladykirk).

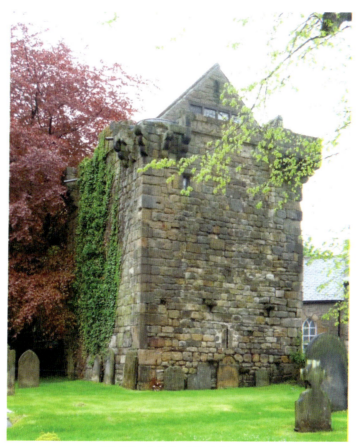

23. Vicar's Pele at Corbridge

Another minor fortification was the vicar's pele, a small pele tower for the vicar. A good example remains in the centre of Corbridge in Northumberland, (postcode NE45 5AW). This small fortified stone tower house dates from 1319 and was the vicarage for the nearby church until the early 17th century.

Some historians have suggested that vicar's peles were not just designed to protect the vicar from reivers. Vicars were often unpopular with their congregations, and at times might have required protection from their flock! Fortified churches and vicar's peles were much more common in England than Scotland.

5. THE BORDER ABBEYS AND KEY RELIGIOUS MONUMENTS

The Abbeys

In the 12th century under King David I there was a flowering of religious orders in Scotland, which resulted in the birth of four abbeys in the eastern Borders. David founded religious houses at Kelso (1128 – Tironensian order), Melrose (1136 – Cistercian order), and Jedburgh (1138 - Augustinian order). His example encouraged his nobles, and in 1150 Hugh de Morville, Lord of Lauderdale and Constable of Scotland, founded Dryburgh Abbey for the Premonstratensian order. The Abbeys were sometimes used by monarchs to reward relatives or supporters, as they could be very lucrative appointments. Therefore James V, for example, arranged for two of his illegitimate infant sons to be made abbots of Melrose and Kelso. James had at least nine illegitimate children, and he died aged 30. If he had lived a long life much of the Scottish population might have descended from him! He would certainly have run out of abbeys.

The abbeys were magnificent. Some would argue that they were too magnificent, and that the king and abbots should have spent more of their funds caring for and supporting their flocks, rather than lavishing vast amounts of treasure on these buildings. Nonetheless, they did create some glorious buildings, and much remains for us to appreciate and enjoy.

The location of the Border abbeys was one of their great weaknesses, standing as they did on main invasion routes into Scotland. Some historians argue that the location was also one reason for their existence. For example, King David I may have had the magnificent Jedburgh Abbey built so close to the border in order to show the English king how rich and powerful Scotland was.

Most of the Border abbeys were destroyed and rebuilt several times in the centuries of intermittent warfare that followed Edward I's attempt to take over Scotland in the late 1200s. The abbeys were well endowed with land holdings and could usually afford to rebuild. However, the "Rough Wooing" from 1543 to 1550 proved to be their end, and they were not fully repaired after they were badly damaged by the marauding English armies. In any event if the English enemy hadn't destroyed them, the Scots may well have done so themselves during the Protestant Reformation, which reached its peak in 1560. The Scots certainly destroyed many of their other abbeys and cathedrals. Between the English and the Scots, much beauty and history was lost forever.

Melrose Abbey
Postcode TD6 9LG

There has been a religious house at Melrose since the 7th century, but the present abbey is one of several foundations that owe their existence to King David I. Around 1136 King David asked the Cistercian order at its magnificent Rievaulx Abbey in Yorkshire to send monks to found a daughter house at Melrose, which he lavishly endowed.

24. Melrose Abbey.

The ruins are beautiful - Melrose has gained a new type of beauty through its partial destruction. Some of the abbey stands to roof height, and there are substantial foundations remaining of the other monastic buildings. Don't miss the gargoyles on the south side of the church. These include a calf with wings, and a very odd pig playing the bagpipes!

Robert the Bruce asked that his heart be interred at Melrose, and in 1921 workmen digging to lay drains discovered a lead casket containing the remains of a heart. This was reinterred, but the casket was rediscovered during archaeological investigations in 1996. The casket was not opened, but reinterred for a second time in June 1998. There is now a plinth in the abbey grounds over the place where the heart was reinterred.

Melrose is an attractive town, and a good starting point to walk in the Eildon Hills, triple peaks just south of Melrose. They rise to 1385 feet (422 metres), and the view from the top certainly justifies the walk. At the top of North Hill there are the remains of an ancient habitation and a substantial rampart.

The Borders Regional Council has produced an excellent booklet describing local walks, available **at** http://www.scotBorders.gov.uk/downloads/ file/ 407/ paths_around_melrose. The Regional Council's booklet includes the following historical background to the Eildon Hills walk:

"In the 10th century BC, Bronze Age people built circular huts, enclosed by a rampart 1.5km in circumference, on North Hill. Nearly 300 hut platforms survive implying that people assembled here in large numbers although there is no convenient water supply and weather conditions can be severe. Although traditionally regarded as one of Scotland's two largest hill forts, the huge enclosure may have been mainly symbolic and, therefore, it is unlikely that a permanent settlement existed here. More probably, it was a focus for communal gatherings and may have provided an opportunity for the dispersed population to meet for ceremonial occasions." Basically, they think it was a sort of stadium.

There was also a Roman signal station near the top. The walk is well worth it.

At the bottom of the peaks at Newsteads are the remains of a major Roman fort called Trimontium. There isn't much to see above ground now, but walking on the way-marked trail round the fort site is a pleasant way to spend a couple of hours.

Dryburgh Abbey

Postcode TD6 0RQ

25. Dryburgh Abbey.

Dryburgh is only 8 miles (13 km) from Melrose by car, and shorter as the crow flies. It is in a rural site, not attached to a town. Situated on a bend in the River Tweed, in well-kept grounds adorned with mature trees, it is in the most attractive situation of all the Border abbeys, and is where Sir Walter Scott the author chose to be buried.

There is a less deserving man buried in the ruins of Dryburgh Abbey - Field Marshall Sir Douglas Haig. Haig led the British Army during much of the First World War, and after the war lived at Bemersyde, a Haig clan property a few miles from the abbey. Guidebooks make much of the fact that he is buried with a simple army tombstone which was similar to that of a common soldier. But Historic Scotland has had the audacity to display the following message:

"Douglas Haig was noted for ingenuity and enterprise during his military career".

When I grew up in the west coast of Scotland in the 1950s and 60s, it was common to use the phrase "as black as the Earl Haig's waistcoat" to describe something evil. Under Haig's command hundreds of thousands of men died in hopeless attacks against German barbed wire and machine guns. Scotland suffered bitterly, as in the absence of other opportunities many Scots became career soldiers and so there were a disproportionate number of Scots in the army from the beginning of the war.

Haig spent much of his military career as a cavalryman, a member of the socially elite branch of the army. His wife had been lady-in-waiting to Queen Alexandra, Edward VII's wife. His social status, rather than his ability, undoubtedly contributed to his rise to the top, although to be fair that was standard practice in the army at the time and no doubt still is. Haig's training and thinking as a cavalryman meant that his skills were obsolete in a 20th century European war. He did not have the background to quickly understand a modern war involving the latest technology. Whilst he did introduce new tactics eventually, to say he lead with "ingenuity and enterprise" goes too far.

Jedburgh Abbey and Town
Postcode TD8 6JQ

26. Jedburgh Abbey.

Jedburgh, now a town of about 4000 people, is on the main A68 road between Edinburgh and Newcastle. Its major Augustinian abbey was founded by King David I of Scotland, and is sited above the Jed Water in the centre of Jedburgh. There had been a religious site there for several centuries before King David I founded a priory in 1138. The priory was promoted to become an abbey around 1150. The building complex was something of a vanity project on King David's behalf – he wanted to display the culture and sophistication of Scotland by building a magnificent abbey.

The abbey was built at a time of peace and prosperity. But as Jedburgh is only 10 miles (16 km) from the English border, it was inevitable that it would be embroiled in border wars and history. So when peace turned to war its location on this strategic route made it particularly susceptible to English attack. It was damaged on a number of occasions. In 1544 and 1545 it was very badly damaged, and in 1547 the abbey complex was fortified by a French force, which was fighting on behalf of the Scots against the English. The abbey complex was never rebuilt after that, although part of the abbey church was used as a church for the local community for some time.

What remains? The main abbey church remains up to the roof, a magnificent Romanesque and Gothic building, and one of the most complete in the U.K. However, much of the monks' domestic buildings are in ruins. Historic Scotland has a visitors' centre containing an informative display, describing the history of the complex.

In the town Mary, Queen of Scots' house (Postcode TD8 6EN), a tower house where Mary stayed in 1566, is now a museum.

About 2 miles (3 km) south of Jedburgh in an attractive location is Ferniehirst castle (Postcode TD8 6NX), the home of the Ferniehirst branch of the Kerr family. The present building largely dates from 1596, and supersedes a 1496 tower house, which was involved in numerous conflicts. As its website proclaims "It was sacked by the English in 1523, attacked and retaken in 1549 with the help of the French and captured by the English once again in 1570. In 1593 the castle was almost completely demolished by James VI as punishment for the then laird assisting his enemies."

Affluent Kerrs visiting the area may be interested in staying in the castle, which has been newly refurbished and has an accommodation wing with six bedrooms for hire. See Ferniehirst's website for more details http://www.ferniehirst.com. The castle is open to visitors in July.

Kelso and Its Abbey
Postcode TD5 7JF

27. Kelso Abbey.

Kelso is an attractive town with a cobbled square, reputed to be the biggest in Scotland, with five cobbled streets leading into it. It doesn't make enough of itself – when I visited on a beautiful day in May I expected to see cafes and restaurants, with their tables spilling out into the square. I was disappointed – the square was largely used as a car park.

Near the centre of Kelso are the remains of Kelso Abbey. The abbey was at its peak one of the most spectacular in Scotland, but now is rather the worst for wear, with much of its once extensive grounds built over and incorporated in Kelso town. As can been seen in the picture, it was built almost like a fortress, a good idea in such a dangerous area. Founded, like so many Scottish abbeys by King David I, it was within sight of Roxburgh Castle, and therefore bound to attract the attention of an invading English army. James II was killed in 1460 when a canon exploded beside him when he was trying to retake Roxburgh Castle from the English invaders, and his nine year old son was hurriedly crowned James III in the abbey.

However its end came in 1545 when the abbey was destroyed in the "rough wooing" of Henry VIII. As Scotland became Protestant in 1560, the abbey was not rebuilt.

The Border Abbeys Cycling and Walking Routes

The four abbeys are linked together for cyclists by the 55 mile (88 km) Borders cycle route. An experienced cyclist could cycle 55 miles in a day. However, I recommend allotting a minimum of three days to this expedition, to give you enough time to take in the abbeys and the many other main historic attractions in the towns and villages that you pass on this 55 mile trail. There is also a 68 mile (109 km) walking route. See www.ourscottishborders.com/visit/activities/cycling for more details of the cycling route, and www.scotborders.gov.uk/directory_record/7470/borders_abbeys_way for the walking route. Googling will find further sites which include these routes.

Anglo Saxon Crosses

Bewcastle
Postcode CA6 6PS

28. Bewcastle's very ruined castle.

Bewcastle is about 10 miles (16 km) south of the border and 7 miles (11 km) north of Hadrian's Wall. There are the remains of a Roman fort, built around the same time as Hadrian's Wall as an outpost and centre for scouting and reconnaissance, and presumably to protect a Romanized area north of the wall. The Roman fort was destroyed in AD 343 when Hadrian's Wall was overrun, and after being rebuilt it was abandoned by the Romans in AD 367.

The Normans invaded England in 1066, but it took them some time to take over the north. In 1092, about the same time that they started to build Carlisle Castle, the Normans are thought to have built an earth and timber castle at Bewcastle within the old Roman defenses. In the 13th century they replaced it with a stone castle, the remains of which can still be seen. The castle was a forward outpost for the Warden of the English West March, guarding entry to England via the wild area adjoining Bewcastle, known as the Bewcastle Waste. The Bewcastle Waste was often used by the reivers of Liddesdale in their raids.

For me though, the main reason to visit Bewcastle is to see the Anglo-Saxon cross standing in St Cuthbert's churchyard. Although now missing its crossbar and tip, the cross still stands about 14.5 feet (4.4 metres) high. The cross is believed to date from the late 7th or first half of the 8th century, and contains both reliefs and writing in the runic alphabet. This is a form of writing used by old Germanic languages, and at one time was common in Northern Europe. But it was progressively superseded in the 1st millennium by Latin script, until it had disappeared by about 1000AD.

This, together with a cross of similar antiquity in Ruthwell in Dumfriesshire, is of major historic and artistic importance. Nicholas Pevesner, the noted architectural historian comment on the crosses "The crosses of Bewcastle and Ruthwell ... are the greatest achievement of their date in the whole of Europe."

It is surprising that such an important monument stands outside in the churchyard, open to the elements, and not surprisingly the runic inscriptions have become worn, and are now difficult to interpret. The Bewcastle website (**www.Bewcastle.com**) speculates that their style looks to Northumbria, and beyond there to Rome and Syria, rather than to Galloway and Ireland.

The crosses are likely to date from after 675 when this area (formerly known as Rheged) had come under Northumbrian control, and when Benedict Biscop brought masons from Syria to build his new monastery at Monkwearmouth/Jarrow. Syria, which is again undergoing awful conflict at the time of writing, must have seemed almost a world away from the wilds of the north west of England in the first millennium. However the Bewcastle website speculates that that the Syrian link is not surprising when we learn that many monks and craftsmen fled persecution there and went to Rome, producing five Popes and also a great reforming Archbishop of Canterbury, Theodore of Tarsus, around this time.

The west face of the cross shows John the Baptist holding the Lamb of God at the top. Below John is Christ being recognized by the animals of the wilderness, and at the bottom of the cross there is some controversy amongst experts as to who the figure is. It could be an Anglo-Saxon nobleman, or alternatively St John the Evangelist. For more details, see the Bewcastle website.

29. Bewcastle Cross.

Ruthwell Cross
Postcode DG1 4NP

30. Ruthwell Cross.

The other major cross in the Borders area is now sited inside the parish church in the small village of Ruthwell in Dumfriesshire, about 35 miles (57 km) from Bewcastle. Like Bewcastle it is also from the Anglo-Saxon Jarrow-Monkwearmouth school of sculpture. It dates from the same time, or perhaps a decade or two later than the Bewcastle Cross. At that time the Northumbrian kingdom had spread as far as Dumfriesshire, and even into Galloway. In addition to religious sculptures, the cross contains inscription in both Latin and the runic alphabet.

This 18 ft (5.2 metres) cross has had an eventful history. In 1640, the Scottish Kirk (church) was fiercely Protestant and strongly opposed to the Catholic Church whose religious worship in their view included craven images. The Scottish Kirk decreed that all idolatrous monuments made for religious purposes should be destroyed. So the cross was broken up and the pieces buried in the churchyard, where they stayed for nearly 200 years.

In the 1800s the local minister, the Reverend Henry Duncan, appreciated the significance and beauty of the cross. He paid for it to be restored and badly broken or missing pieces replaced. In 1823 it was erected in the gateway to his manse.

In the later 1800s there was concern about the effect of the weather on such an important historic monument. Therefore a small extension was added to the church just to house the cross.

6. STATELY HOMES AND THEIR OWNERS

Abbotsford and Sir Walter Scott

Postcode TD6 9BQ

31. Abbotsford House.

Sir Walter Scott was one of Britain's best known writers in the 19th century, and helped to invent the historic fiction genre of novels. He used his considerable royalties to rebuild and transform an old farmhouse called Cartleyhole into the neo-Baronial extravaganza of Abbotsford. However in the longer term probably his greatest achievement was to bring Scotland together by breaking down the barrier between highlander and lowlander.

Scott was born in Edinburgh in 1771 to a prominent legal family that originated in the Borders, and had a reiving history. One of his ancestors was William Scott of Harden, who to escape the gallows after a bungled cattle raid was forced to marry Agnes Murray of Elibank, also known as muckle-mouthed Meg, no beauty! (She is supposed to have had a kindly disposition though, so William may not done badly out of the deal).

Walter contracted polio as a boy, and was sent to live in the Borders with his grandparents at Sandyknowe farm, next to Smailholm Tower which they also owned. Smailholm Tower is pictured on the cover of this book, and described on page 35. The countryside was considered a much healthier place to live than Edinburgh. This was just before the building of Edinburgh's New Town, and the population was then concentrated in the Old Town, a dirty, insanitary and overcrowded place. Six of Scott's brothers and sisters died in infancy. Scott recovered from polio, but was left with a limp. But his stay in and frequent visits to the Borders left him with a love for the area, and a deep knowledge of border folklore and ballads.

In Edinburgh he followed the family career of lawyer, and also started writing. As well as documenting border ballads and writing poetry, Scott helped invent the historical novel, setting fictional characters and adventures within genuine historical events. He is now out of fashion, as his style is verbose by current standards, and some of his stories such as Ivanhoe and Rob Roy almost innocent and romantic, rather than realistic. But in his time he was a world famous writer, who created an image of Scotland through his writing and other activities which still exists today.

Scott was appointed the sheriff of Selkirkshire, which is the government appointed legal officer, effectively a judge. He moved to a farmhouse near Galashiels, which he renamed Abbotsford and extended over six years into a major country seat for an affluent Scottish gentleman.

Abbotsford incorporates a range of styles and objects Scott collected from historic sites throughout Scotland. He loved Abbotsford, and it is where he wrote most of his Waverley novels. He said of Abbotsford:

"It is a kind of conundrum castle to be sure, and I have great pleasure in it, for while it pleases a fantastic person in style and manner of its architecture it has all the comforts of a commodious habitation".

Scott was active in politics as a Tory. He organized a search in Edinburgh castle which in 1818 found the lost Scottish crown jewels. These had been locked away in a chest in the castle in 1707 when the treaty of union was signed with England and forgotten for 100 years! He received a knighthood for finding them.

Another major achievement as a political fixer was to choreograph the visit of King George IV to Scotland in 1822. This was the first visit of a reigning monarch since 1650. George was portly and dissolute, a spendthrift with many mistresses during his life. A peacock, George saw himself as a leader of fashion. Scott built on the image of the highlander to create a theatrical Scottish image for the visit. He took the highlander's plaid, which following the 1745 rebellion had been proscribed until 1782, and created a much more colourful tartan formal dress. A separate tartan for each clan was developed. King George certainly bought into this, wearing a kilt and full highland dress over his portly frame at some events during the visit.

As organizer, Scott laid out and published a dress code for the main events. The height of the visit was a grand ball. Scott specified that gentlemen attending the ball, if not entitled to wear military uniform, should wear his elaborate version of "highland dress". Before the event lowlanders would have considered the authentic, less elaborate highland dress to be the dress of highland "tramps and thieves". Suddenly everyone attending the ball was clamoring to get a kilt. In one evening an exaggerated version of highland dress became the must have fashion item for the Scottish upper class and anyone with any aspirations to be upper class. Through his writing and the development of a common formal dress code Scott helped to break down the age long gulf between highlander and lowlander. Previously they had almost been two separate nationalities – now they were all Scots with a unified heritage.

Scott's literary output was prodigious, at his peak producing two books a year. To some extent he was forced into this. He was a partner in a printing and publishing firm that went bankrupt in a depression of the time, and rather than go bankrupt he wrote quickly to pay off his creditors.

Scott used his considerable income from writing to build Abbotsford, and from shortly after his death it has been open to the public. It contains an impressive collection of weapons, armour, Scott's library and a host of historic relics. It is a shrine to Scott, his work and his vision of Scotland. See www.scottsabbotsford.com for more details.

However, although he did much for Scotland, some of his views would today be seen as archaic and reactionary. Shortly before his death he argued strongly against the Reform Act 1832, which inter alia reduced the property requirement to vote, and therefore extended the electoral franchise from 5000 large landowners in Scotland to about 65,000 electors, a small move forward in increasing the franchise. Scott's reputation was damaged because of the stance he took, and he did not prevent the Reform Act being passed.

It is possible to be critical of Scott, and to see him as the developer of an overly sentimental and tacky Scottishness. A fairer interpretation is that Scott used the fascinating, and at times heroic history of Scotland's battle to retain its independence from a powerful and often aggressive neighbor, to strengthen a Scottish identity. The sentimental Scottish identity Scott helped promote brought the people of Scotland together in a way they hadn't been before.

Scott died in 1832 and is buried beside his wife amongst the stately remains of Dryburgh Abbey.

Drumlanrig Castle and the Douglases

Postcode DG3 4AQ

32. Drumlanrig Castle.

Drumlanrig Castle is about 17 miles (27 km) north of Dumfries. Drumlanrig is a palace rather than a castle, set in a carefully laid out estate surrounded by rolling border hills. It was the seat of the Douglases of Drumlanrig.

Sir James Douglas was the right hand man of Robert the Bruce. For the support given to Bruce in the wars of independence he received the Drumlanrig estate in Nithsdale. In the 14th century the Douglases built a tower house there. The Douglas fortunes waxed and waned in the 15th and 16th centuries, but in the second half of the 17th with the return of Charles II they were in the ascendant again.

In the 1680s William Douglas, 3rd Earl of Queensberry, was the most powerful man in Scotland below the king. From 1682 to 1686 he was Lord High Treasurer of Scotland. In 1684 William was made a Duke. As his power increased he wanted a home to reflect his status, and in 1679 he commissioned the building of the present castle/palace, built in local pink sandstone and incorporating the old tower house. The cost was enormous, and the Duke may well have come to regret it. He sealed the building accounts in an envelope, and is reported to have said "the deil pike out the ein wha looks herein" (the devil pick out the eye of anyone who looks inside).

In 1810, on the death of the 4th Duke of Queensberry, the title and Drumlanrig passed to the Duke of Buccleuch, who is now called the Duke of Buccleuch and Queenberry. The 3rd Duke of Buccleuch was great-grandson of the 2nd Duke of Queensberry.

Drumlanrig contains innumerable works of art, including Rembrandt's An Old Woman Reading, and works by Thomas Gainsborough, Alan Ramsay and Sir Joshua Reynolds. It also has cabinets by the 17th century French master Andre Charles Boulle, and important antique tapestries and porcelain.

Other Stately Homes

The Borders has a number of other mansions, including:

Bowhill House
Postcode TD7 5ET

We have come across Scott of Buccleuch several times in this text. Bowhill is now the family home of the family. The land was given to the family in 1322 by King Robert the Bruce in recognition of their loyalty.

The Buccleuch website states that the Buccleuch name originates from the 10th century, when legend has it that King Kenneth III was hunting in a deep ravine or 'cleuch' in the heart of the forest. A young buck became cornered and charged towards the unarmed King. A young man named John Scott seized the buck by the antlers and wrestled it to the ground, saving the King's life. From that day, the Scotts were referred to as Buck Cleuch (the 'buck from the ravine').

The present house replaced a modest 18th century country house. The imposing Bowhill we see today is mainly 19th century, and is the work of several architects including William Atkinson, William Burn and David Bryce. Sir Walter Scott, a kinsman and frequent visitor, admired the house so much he christened it 'Sweet Bowhill' in his famous poem, 'The Lay of the Last Minstrel'.

The house contains superb art treasures, including 18th century hand-painted Chinese wallpapers, numerous famous paintings and thousands of books.

Floors Castle
Postcode TD5 7SF

Floors castle is a palace rather than a castle, and is probably the largest inhabited palace in Britain.

It was designed by two of Scotland's leading architects. William Adam designed the building in 1720s for the 1st Duke of Roxburghe, a Ker (or Kerr), one of the best known Borders families. In the 1830s the architect William Playfair, famous for developing part of Edinburgh's New Town, was commissioned to remodel the castle. Playfair added an elaborate fairy-tale roofscape, and a grand ballroom.

The direct Ker line died out in 1756. After a very, very long and expensive legal case involving competing distant relatives, the House of Lords decided for Sir James Innes, who took the title of the 5th Duke and adopted the name of Innes Ker.

Thirlestane Castle
Postcode TD2 6RU

Thirlestane Castle is another palace, built on the site of an older fortification. In a prominent position 28 miles (45km) south of Edinburgh and three miles (5km) east of Lauder, the fortification that preceded Thirlestane was strategically situated to protect Edinburgh from invaders approaching via Lauderdale. The first stage of the modern building, the main block, was built around 1590 by the 1st Lord Maitland of Thirlestane, then Lord Chancellor of Scotland.

The second stage was built by Lord Maitland's grandson, the Duke of Lauderdale. This old rogue was described by a contemporary Lord as 'insolent, imperious, flattering and dissembling, and having no impediment of honor to restrain him from doing anything that might satisfy any of his passions'. He was of course a politician by profession. The Duke wanted his house to retain the look of a castle, but to have the magnificence of a palace. The inside was remodeled, elaborate plasterwork added, and two towers added to the front of the building. The third major remodeling occurred in 1840 when the 9th Duke of Lauderdale added two large wings to the castle, to create more space, and an elaborate roof and turrets.

7. RAILWAYS IN THE BORDERS

Progressing Back to 1849!

September 2015 was a historic month for the Borders. Part of the Waverley Line, as far as Tweedbank beyond Galashiels, was officially reopened by Queen Elizabeth II, (or Elizabeth I of Scotland, since Scotland has not had an Elizabeth as queen before).

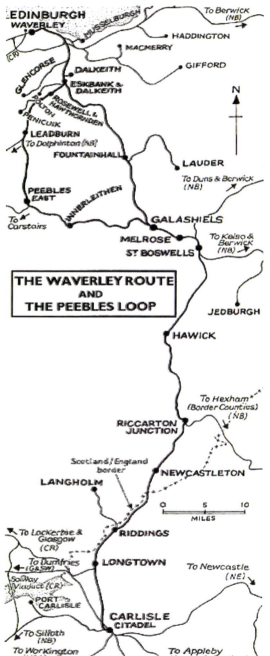

33. *The Waverley Line and the adjoining rail network as was. Map drawn by Alan Young.*

The train line, which was first opened in 1849, had been a major artery into the Borders until it was closed during the "Beeching" cuts. The line was the main Edinburgh, Galashiels, Hawick, and Newcastleton to Carlisle route, and was named after the Waverley series of novels by Sir Walter Scott. The map shows how it intersected with a whole range of local lines, most of which no longer exist. This gave these towns access to the whole UK rail network. In the second half of the 19th and first half of the 20th centuries the Borders had a whole spider's web of railway lines linking all Borders towns and villages of any significance. Apart from the east and west coast mainlines, and a line from Carlisle via Dumfries to Glasgow, all were swept away in the Beeching cuts in the 1960s. This left much of the area more isolated than it had been fifty years before.

The last train before the closure of the line was an Edinburgh to London overnight sleeper on 5 January 1969. This was held up at Newcastleton in Liddesdale, the centre of reiving country, when the minister and his parishioners padlocked the level crossing gates in protest at the closure of the line.

The direct line from Edinburgh to Tweedbank, a new station between Galashiels and Melrose, is the section that was reopened in September 2015.

The original Waverley Line was opened in stages, the Edinburgh to Galashiels stage being fully opened on 20 January 1849. Hawick was reached on 1 November 1849. However because of a cholera epidemic in Hawick the celebrations, which usually took place when the railway reached a town, were very subdued.

The line was very demanding for engines because of its steep ascents and descents. The Edinburgh to Galashiels section involves going over the Falahill summit, at almost 900 feet above sea level. The line closer to Carlisle, which isn't part of the current redevelopment, involved a long climb up to Whitrope summit at 1006ft (307 metres), and a trip though Whitrope Tunnel, a 1,208 yard (1,105 metre) tunnel, the fourth longest tunnel in Britain and now a grade B listed building.

Two things are worth doing. Firstly, take a journey on this new line. You will see views of the Borders you can't see by road. Secondly, for rail buffs, or people who just want to learn more about the line, visit Whitrope Heritage Centre (Postcode TD9 9TY). Whitrope Heritage Centre is based in two railway carriages at Whitrope siding, just off the B6399 between Hawick and Newcastleton. Here a team of dedicated enthusiasts, the Waverley Route Heritage Association, are working to save and restore as much as they can.

The Heritage Centre, on a stretch of open moorland, contains a selection of old railway relics from the Borders' railways, some old rolling stock, and many old photographs and a display on how the railway was built. It may be possible to take a short train journey along part of the almost 1 mile (1.6 km) of railway track they have restored. Adjoining the exhibition coach is a buffet coach, where you can enjoy a cup of tea in a 1960s carriage. Check their website though, **www.wrha.org.uk**, to confirm what will be open before making a journey to the centre.

8. PLANNING YOUR VISIT

Getting to the Borders

If coming by train, you can start your visit in either Carlisle or Berwick-upon-Tweed, which are on the West Coast and East Coast main lines respectively. And since September 2015 there has also been the option of travelling by train from Edinburgh on the newly reopened stretch of the Waverley Line (see chapter 7). When you arrive in the Borders it would be best to hire a car to see some of the key sites, as public transport is limited in rural areas.

If you drive to the area, Carlisle and Berwick-upon-Tweed are also good routes in, and two of the routes invading armies have taken for the last two millennia, and probably longer! Alternatively you can drive up the A68 from Newcastle if travelling from the south. This takes you close to the best stretches of Hadrian's Wall, and on to Jedburgh and Kerr territory, in the past another invasion route.

Throughout the text I have included the postcode of the historic sites mentioned in the book, to help visitors with smartphones or satellite navigation systems in their cars. Postcodes in the countryside can cover a wider area than in towns, so if you arrive at a postcode and can't immediately see the site, please just search a little further. There isn't a map in the book – nothing could compare to google maps or some of the other computer mapping systems. However, two paper maps are recommended in the bibliography.

Arranging Accommodation

The bibliography recommends two maps which will help in planning. Local tourist information centers and their internet sites have a range of accommodation. See:

For Scotland http://www.visitscotland.com/accommodation/

For Cumbria in northwest England http://www.visitcumbria.com/tourist-information-centres/

For Northumberland in northeast England http://www.visitnorthumberland.com/

Also worth checking are www.Tripadivsor.com and www.booking.com. Internet sites now provide a better guide to accommodation than a book can.

Organising Your Visit

The following tables group the key 25 sites in the text with their postcodes, and identify suitable bases in the area for the visitor.

http://www.visithadrianswall.co.uk/ and the tourist information sites referred to above provide a good choice of accommodation when visiting Hadrian's Wall. If you are happy to stay a little further afield, Brampton is a suitable base for both the wall and the Carlisle area sites.

Chesters Fort and Museum	NE46 4EU	See Chapter 2 for Hadrian's Wall
Housesteads Fort	NE47 6NN	
Vindolanda	NE47 7JN	
Walltown, and the Roman Army Museum	CA8 7JB.	

Carlisle is the obvious place to stay to visit the following sites. However if you want a more attractive rural location, I recommend the small town of Brampton, about ten miles (16km) east of Carlisle.

Carlisle Castle	CA3 8UR	Page 29
Bewcastle	CA6 6PS	P 43
Newton Arlosh Church	CA7 5ET	P 36
Hermitage Castle	TD9 0LU	P 25
Gilnockie Tower	DG14 0XD	P 34

The Dumfries area is the obviously place to base yourself to visit the following sites. And if you are interested in Robert Burns, Dumfries has many associations with Burns and a museum, the Robert Burns Centre.

Ruthwell Cross	DG1 4NP	Page 46
Caerlaverock Castle	DG1 4RU	P 24
Drumlanrig Castle	DG3 4AQ	P 49
Orchardton Tower	DG7 1QH	P 24
Threave Castle	DG7 1TJ	P 22

This central section is the honeypot of the Borders. I love Melrose and Kelso, and either of these places would make a good base to visit these sites. Jedburgh too has a lot of accommodation. Kelso is the most central location for the sites in question.

Thirlestane Castle	TD2 6RU	Page 50
Kelso and Its Abbey	TD5 7JF	P 42
Smailholm Tower	TD5 7PG	P 35
Floors Castle	TD5 7SF	P 50
Hume Castle	TD5 7TR	P 28
Cessford Castle	TD5 8EG	P 27
Dryburgh Abbey	TD6 0RQ	P 40
Abbotsford	TD6 9BQ	P 47
Melrose Abbey	TD6 9LG	P 38
Bowhill House	TD7 5ET	P 50
Jedburgh Abbey	TD8 6JQ	P 41

The following two sites could be visited from the Kelso, but if you want to base yourself closer, Berwick-upon-Tweed and Norham will both have accommodation.

Norham Castle	TD15 2JY	Page 31
Berwick-upon-Tweed	TD15 1NA	P 33

9. THE KEY BORDER FAMILIES

On the Scottish side the main surnames were Armstrong, Beattie, Bell, Burns/Bourne, Croser/Crosier, Douglas, Elliot, Gordon, Graham, Hepburn, Home/Hume, Irving/Irvine, Jardine, Johnstone, Kerr, Little, Maxwell, Nixon, Oliver, Pringle, Rutherford, Scott and Swinton.   English surnames included Charlton/Carleton, Dacre, Fenwick, Forster/Foster, Graham, Storey, Musgrave, Nixon, Ridley and Robson. There are many spelling for some of the above names.   Country of origin wasn't clear-cut; some surnames could extend to either side of the border. The Grahams for example were a cross-border clan.

Many people in an area might have the same surname, and there are a limited number of first names. There were several solutions to ensure there was less duplication in names. One was to use colorful and expressive nicknames, based on some physical or personality characteristic. For example Wee Jock Elliot, Fingerless Will Nixon. An alternative was to incorporate the man's property or place of origin in the name, such as Kinmont Willie, or Jock of the Park. Further options were to include a mark of rank, such as Sim the Laird, or to include the father's first name, such as Willie's Sim.

I have mentioned previously that the peoples on both sides of the border are ethnically the same. However in recent years they have displayed an interesting difference in their feelings of kinship. The Scots now show a much greater interest in the history of their families, and the many clan societies in the UK and throughout the world are evidence of this. English surnames do not seem to have the equivalent "clan" identity.

Armstrong

There is a legend that the Armstrong clan originated from a knight called Fairbairn, who lifted the King of Scotland up onto his horse after the King's horse had been killed in battle. The king granted him the title of Armstrong, and land in the Borders.

The Armstrongs' main power base was in Liddesdale and Annandale, and at their peak they could summon 3000 riders, effectively an army. They were one of the most powerful families in the area, and were notorious reivers. So notorious that, as mentioned in chapter 3, a young King James V hung a large group of Armstrongs led by Johnnie Armstrong of Gilnockie, at Carlenrig, about 10 miles (16 km) southwest of Hawick. Another infamous incident described in chapter 3 was Kinmont Willie Armstrong's jailbreak from Carlisle Castle.

The Armstrongs made a giant leap for mankind in 1969 when Neil Armstrong, whose ancestors originated from Langholm in the Borders, became the first man to walk on the moon.

Bell

A prominent West March reiving clan, often a client and ally of clan Douglas. The name derived from the French bel, meaning good looking. The Bells' main base was in the parish of Middlebie, six miles north east of Annan. There were also some Bells in England, close to the border. Several Bells were involved in the raid which freed Kinmont Willie Armstrong from Carlisle Castle.

Famous Bells include Alexander Graham Bell, the developer of the telephone who was born in Edinburgh and moved to Canada. Dr Joseph Bell taught Sir Arthur Conan Doyle medicine in Edinburgh, and Dr Bell's methodical and forensic analysis of data inspired Conan Doyle when creating Sherlock Holmes.

Douglas

The Douglases were widely spread, but with concentrations in Nithsdale, Galloway, and around Hawick. Whilst the Douglases did little reiving themselves, they were heavily involved in the politics of the Borders (and Scotland). The name originated from the Gaelic dubh glais meaning black water. The Douglases controlled the major castles of Hermitage and Threave for many years, and from Threave in the 14th century a Douglas was Warden of the Scottish West March.

The Douglases were for a long time, and particularly in the 13th and 14th centuries, the second most powerful clan in Scotland, second only to the Stewart clan of the king. The Douglases rose to prominence again in the 16th century, when for three years from 1525 Archibald Douglas, the 6th Earl of Angus, in practice ruled Scotland. Douglas, who was James V's step-father, held the young James V prisoner and ruled in James' name. Later in the second half of the 17th century the Douglas fortunes, which had waxed and waned, were in the ascendant again. One of their castles, Drumlanrig in Nithsdale (postcode DG3 4AQ), originally a tower house, was transformed into a palace in a major building programme between 1679 and 1689. It is now a major tourist attraction, with many works of art.

Elliot

There are many different spellings of the name, some significantly different, such as Ellwood. The Elliots were based in Liddesdale like their sometimes rivals, sometimes allies, the Armstrongs. Like the Armstrongs they were notorious reivers, gangsters of the border Middle March. Elliot chiefs were sometimes appointed Captains of Hermitage Castle. See Hepburn below for an incident when James Hepburn, 4th earl of Bothwell, was the Captain.

Gordon

The Gordon clan originates in the Borders, where there is a village called Gordon. Their seat was in a castle near the village. The castle was replaced by Greenknowe tower, a late 16th century pele tower now under the care of Historic Scotland. The clan head was given significant landholdings in north east Scotland by Robert the Bruce as a reward for their involvement in the wars of independence, and to help Bruce control the unruly north east. There they became Earls, then Marquis of Huntly, and then Dukes of Gordon, a dukedom being the highest rank in the British peerage. Their fortunes grew in the north east, where the clan chief was referred to as the "Cock of the North", and the border Gordons became the junior branch of the family.

Graham

Like the Gordons, the Grahams had several seats, including Dalkeith in Midlothian and Kincardine Castle in central Scotland. Many of the more disreputable elements of the clan lived in the "Debatable Land" in the Borders.

They were a cross border clan, with substantial numbers in England. They appear to have been particularly disreputable and troublesome, which is quite an accolade, considering the competition they were up against! Therefore many of the border Grahams were deported to Ireland by James VI, when he became James 1 of England. Their deportation and sense of loss is commemorated in the song "Sweet Ennerdale".

Hepburn

The Hepburns are thought to originate from Northumberland, where there is a ruined but still substantial Hepburn Bastle. This is, in fact, a tower house rather than a bastle. Their rise in Scotland is down to Adam de Hepburne, who was a prisoner of the Earl of March in Scotland, and saved the earl from a runaway horse. In gratitude the Earl granted Hepburne land in Lothian. The Hepburns subsequently became major landowners in Lothian and the Borders. In 1488, for supporting James IV against his father James III, Hepburn of Hailes was made earl of Bothwell.

The most famous Hepburn is James, 4th earl of Bothwell and duke of Orkney, the third husband of Mary, Queen of Scots. He was Captain of Hermitage Castle and responsible for law and order in Liddesdale when Wee Jock Elliot stabbed him during a skirmish. This resulted in Mary, Queen of Scots' famous marathon ride from Jedburgh to Hermitage through bad autumn weather to see her injured paramour in October 1566. Eventually Bothwell became Mary's third husband, in what was a tumultuous marriage to say the least.

Home/or Hume

The Homes were a powerful clan based in Berwickshire in the East March, and were frequently the March Warden. Home is pronounced Hume, and therefore many clan members adopted Hume as their name, to avoid confusion. The first recorded Home is Aidan de Home in the 13th century. The Homes were heavily involved in the Borders wars and in Scottish politics. Like most major families their fortunes waxed and waned. They were involved in the rebellion against James III of Scotland.

In 1513 the Homes were part of James IV's army which was destroyed at the Battle of Flodden, and although unlike much of the Scottish aristocracy Lord Home survived, much of his family did not. In 1516 Lord Home was accused of treason, and he and his brother were executed and their heads displayed on Edinburgh Tollbooth. However the lands and estates were later restored to another brother.

Prominent Humes/Homes include David Hume (1711-1776), the most significant philosopher in what is known as the Scottish enlightenment in the 18th century. He chose to spell his name Hume, to reflect the way that it was pronounced. Henry Homes, who adopted the honorary title of Lord Kames when he became a senior Scottish judge, was another major figure in the Scottish enlightenment, and wrote extensively on the theory of the legal system. In 1777, Lord Kames was one of the panel of judges who ruled that slavery was illegal in Scotland, in the Joseph Knight case.

Sir Alec Douglas Home, (1903-1995), was UK Prime Minister in 1963-64. Sir Alec had to relinquish his title to become Prime Minister, but was later created a life peer as Lord Home of the Hirsel, the Hirsel being the ancestral home.

John Hume, a leading Northern Irish politician, received a Nobel Prize in 1998 for his contribution to the Irish peace process. His great grandfather had emigrated from Scotland to Northern Ireland.

Cardinal Basil Hume, born in Newcastle-upon-Tyne, was head of the Roman Catholic Church in England and Wales in the late 20th century. His father was a Protestant and mother a Roman Catholic.

See also Hume Castle in chapter 4.

Irving/Irvine

Probably deriving from the old English christian name of Erewine or Erwinne, the clan originated in Dumfriesshire and Ayrshire. A William de Irwin was Robert the Bruce's armor bearer. Bruce granted the family an estate at Drum in Aberdeenshire to add to their holdings in the Borders. Because of the geographical separation of the estates, the two families then had little contact. The Border Irvings supported the Johnstones in their long-term feud against the Maxwells, and were heavily involved in Border history.

Jardine

The Jardine motto, "Cave Adsum - Beware, I am here", was borrowed by Sir Walter Scott as the motto of Sir Reginald Front-de-Boeuf in Ivanhoe!

Jardine derives from the French jardin – a garden or orchard. They were Norman knights. A Walfredus de Jardine is recorded in the 1100s as a witness to the charter for the Abbey of Kelso. The Jardines were based near Lockerbie.

For a small clan, the Jardines have had a greater influence on the world than most. In the 1800s a Jardine married the niece of the King of Samoa. However the most famous Jardine was Doctor William Jardine, who after working as a surgeon for the East India company in the early 1800s, set up the trading firm of Jardine Matheson in Hong Kong in the 1820s. In its early days it was heavily involved in supplying opium to the Chinese, I regret to say (opium was legal in the West but not in China at that time). Jardine Matheson became a major trading and financial conglomerate in the Far East and for many years recruited many of its young managers from the Borders.

Johnstone

There are a number of other spellings of the surname, Johnson and Johnston being particularly common.

Johnstone comes from John's toun (town). There were many small communities controlled by someone called John, so the name originated in various parts of Scotland, and particularly Perth, which was originally known as St John's Toun.

In 1296 Sir John Johnstone was one of the signatories to the Ragman's Role, a document which the nobles and major landowners of Scotland signed confirming their allegiance to Edward I of England – they had little choice at the time. Later the Johnstones were loyal to King James in his feud with the powerful Douglas clan, and as a result some of the Douglas land was granted to the Johnstones.

In the Borders the Johnstones were a major reiver clan, based in Annandale and elsewhere in the Scottish West March. In the twisted and complex power dealings of the 15th and 16th centuries, the clan head was often Warden of the West March, responsible to the king for enforcing law and order. Who ensured the Johnstones obeyed the law is not recorded! The Johnstones had major feuds with the Moffats and the Maxwells, other local clans. They frequently competed with the Maxwells for the wardenship, which changed hands between them on several occasions.

Kerr

The Kerrs (also known as Ker, or especially in England as Carr) competed with the Scotts as the major clan of the Scottish Middle March. There were two main branches – Cessford and Ferniehirst, originating from two brothers Ralph and John in the 14th century. The two branches of the family frequently had a difficult relationship throughout the reiving era. Kerrs from either branch were at times Wardens of the Middle March. The Kerrs also had a long term feud with the Scotts (see Two Great Reiver Feuds in chapter 3). See also Cessford Castle, Ferniehirst Castle in chapter 4.

Little

Probably derives from the height of one of the forbearers of the clan. However, I have known several Littles and they are now as tall as anyone else! It is a common name in Upper Eskdale and Ewesdale. They were listed in 1587 as one of the unruly clans of the West March.

Maxwell

Maxwell may originate from Maccus, a Norse Chief who lived in the Tweed area, and who gave his name to Maccus Well, a pool in the river Tweed. In about 1220 Alexander II of Scotland granted the Caerlaverock estate to Sir John de Maccuswell (Maxwell) in order to strengthen the King's influence in Dumfriesshire, between the twin dangers of England and the unruly Galloway clans. And so began the Maxwells' long association with Dumfriesshire. The head of the clan was often Warden of the West March.

Much of Maxwell history intertwines with that of their deadly (in reality, not figuratively speaking), rivals the Johnstones. Please see chapter 3 – The Reivers for details of the famous Maxwell-Johnstone feud.

The Maxwell Fifth Earl of Nithsdale was a Roman Catholic, and a Jacobite sympathizer. He fought for the Jacobite cause in the 1715 rising, and was captured at the Battle of Preston. He was found guilty of treason and sentenced to death. On the night before his execution, he was visited by his wife, her maid and two friends. After supplying the guards with ample money for alcohol to ensure they were too intoxicated to be watchful, the group shaved off Maxwell's beard and he dressed in some women's clothes they had smuggled in. He was then able to walk out of the prison, whilst his wife carried out a sham conversation, which the partly inebriated guards thought was with her husband in the cell. The very gutsy Countess of Nithsdale was then able to walk out of the prison. They escaped to Rome, where they lived for many years.

Nixon

From the son of Nick. Common on both sides of the Border, in Liddesdale and around Bewcastle. The most famous Nixon is of course former American President Nixon. In the Borders reivers novel "The Candlemass Road" by George MacDonald Fraser, the villains are a band of Nixons. And George Macdonald Fraser knew a thing or two about the reivers!

Pringle

Now known for quality knitwear and crisps, the Pringles were a prominent Borders family, and supporters of the powerful Douglas family. The name is a derivation of the old surname Hopringle, from an estate of that name near Stow in the Borders. Robert Pringle was squire to James, Earl of Douglas, who died at the battle of Otterburn in 1388. Robert survived, and the Douglases gave him the lands of Smailholm for his services. The Pringles built Smailholm Tower to provide protection in the dangerous Borders. Flodden claimed five senior Pringles, the clan chief David Pringle and his four sons.

Famous Pringles include Thomas Pringle, who was a border poet and writer, and a major campaigner for the abolition of slavery. The Pringle knitwear company was established by Robert Pringle in the Borders in 1815. The company has been through various owners in recent years, and since 2000 has been owned by S.C. Fang & Sons, a Hong Kong company, with most products now being sourced from Asia. This could be a case study for the decline of the Border textile industry.

Rutherford

Derived from the Old English for cattle ford. A prominent family of the East March. Two Rutherfords appear in the "Ragman's Roll" of 1296.

Although a small border family, the Rutherford's contribution to science is of global significance. Lord Ernest Rutherford, who was born in New Zealand of Border stock, made an enormous contribution to nuclear physics in the early 20th century. Daniel Rutherford discovered nitrogen in Edinburgh in 1772. Daniel Rutherford's half-sister was the mother of Sir Walter Scott, the author. Another Rutherford, Alison Rutherford (Cockburn after her marriage), was related to Sir Walter Scott's mother and was Edinburgh's great society hostesses of the day, and great friends of key Scottish Enlightenment figures such as David Hume. Alison was born near Selkirk and moved to Edinburgh after her marriage. She also wrote the lyrics for one version of "Flowers of the Forest", which commemorates the Scottish defeat at the Battle of Flodden.

Scott

The Scotts were one of the great clans of the Middle March, involved in all sorts of mischief, such as Scott of Buccleuch organising and leading the jail break of Kinmont Willie Armstrong from Carlisle Castle. See chapter 3.

In the 1600's the Scotts went from strength to strength. In favor with the king, the clan chief's land holdings increased until they became one of Scotland's biggest landowners. Anne Scott, the heir to the Scott dynasty (her brother and sister had both died), married King Charles II's favorite illegitimate son, the Duke of Monmouth. Charles had many illegitimate children by a number of mistresses. When Monmouth didn't inherit the crown on the death of Charles II, he led a revolt which was crushed at the Battle of Sedgemoor, and Monmouth was executed. However, his widow Anne was a canny political operator, and managed to avoid having her title and fortune forfeited. It has been said that in three generations the Scotts went from reivers to royalty.

The most famous Scott was of course Sir Walter Scott, the most read author in the world in the early 1800s. He had an abiding love of the Borders, and spent much of his life around Galashiels and Kelso. See chapter 6 for more information.

BIBLIOGRAPHY

There are a range of books on the Borders, many of them focusing on the time of the reivers. Rather than quote an extensive bibliography I have chosen to focus on a few key texts, many of which have their own bibliographies, should you want to read more extensively.

To study the Border and the reivers in more detail:

Fraser, George MacDonald. *The Steel Bonnets.* William Collins 1971. This classic study of the reivers, is well worth reading.

Moffat, Alistair. *The Reivers: the Story of the Border Reivers.* Birlinn Ltd 2008. Also a very good read.

Moffat, Alistair. *The Borders: A History of the Borders from Earliest Times*. A detailed book.

Turnbull, Ronald. *Battle Valleys.* Frances Lincoln Ltd 2012. An excellent photographic exploration of the Borders.

Durham, Keith. *Strongholds of the Border Reivers.* 2008. Osprey Publishing. Particularly useful if you are interested in castles and fortifications. Highly recommended.

Tough, D L W. *The Last Years of a Frontier.* A History of the Borders during the Reign of Elizabeth I. Oxford University Press 1928.

Wider Scottish History

A quick search on Amazon will show that there are many books on this topic. Some of the best are:

Allan, David. *Scottish History: A Complete Introduction.* Teach Yourself Paperback. 2015. Written as a student text, but none the worse for that.

Magnusson, Magnus. *Scotland: The Story of a Nation.* HarperCollins 2001.

Oliver, Neil. *A History of Scotland.* Weidenfeld & Nicolson 2010. An easy to read introduction.

Hadrian's Wall

The wall deserves a whole book on its own. In fact, a series of books. I can thoroughly recommend:

Brabbs, Derry. *Hadrian's Wall*. Frances Lincoln Ltd, 2008

Geldard, Ed. *Hadrian's Wall, Edge of an Empire*. The Crowood Press, 2011.

Both books provide a good overview, and their photographs are stunning.

Maps

The AA's *North of England & Scottish Borders* map provides good coverage of the road network.

In Search of the Border Reivers: An Historical Map and Guide by the UK's Ordnance Survey is well worth getting for its coverage of the reivers period. This provides a very full map of reiver sites, and some excellent information on the border reiver period.

INDEX OF SURNAMES ASSOCIATED WITH THE BORDERS

Where there are similar spellings, only the most common spelling of a surname is used.

Many of the photographs in "Exploring History in the Scottish Borders" can be obtained from www.picfair.com, for printing on your printer, sending to a commercial printer or using as a screen saver. Just search for Ian Douglas in the website's search box, and then click on the photo to see the full photo.

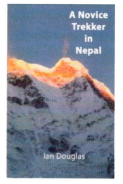

Also by Ian Douglas
A Novice Trekker in Nepal

This is more than just a trekking book, and should be of interest to anyone wanting to learn about this fascinating country. The book describes a trek to the Annapurna Sanctuary in Nepal. As well as being a journal of the author's trek, the book describes the realities of trekking in Nepal for the first time trekker. It explains what the trekker should take on the trek, the type of accommodation he or she will encounter, and other practical matters the first time trekker will find useful. Available in e-book and paper format.

Please see the author's website www.theheritagephotographer.com for updates and details of other publications.

61111030R00040